Managing Yourself for Excellence

How to Become a Can-Do Person

Dr. Beverly Potter

RONIN

Oakland CA

Managing Yourself for Excellence

How to Become a Can-Do Person

Dr. Beverly Potter
docpotter.com

Managing Yourself for Excellence

Copyright 2009: Beverly A. Potter
ISBN: 978-1-57951-089-3

Published by
Ronin Publishing, Inc.
PO Box 22900
Oakland, CA 94609
www.roninpub.com

Production:

Cover Design:	design@BrianGroppe.com.
Book Design:	Beverly A. Potter.

Fonts

Venus—Chank
Comic Sans—Microsoft

Library of Congress Card Number: 2009904258
Distributed to the book trade by PGW/Perseus

Other Books by Docpotter

Beyond Conscious
What Happens After Death

Overcoming Job Burnout
How to Renew Enthusiasm for Work

The Worrywart's Companion
Twenty-One Ways to Soothe Yourself & Worry Smart

From Conflict to Cooperation
How to Mediate a Dispute

Finding a Path with a Heart
How to Go from Burnout to Bliss

Preventing Job Burnout
A Workbook

The Way of the Ronin
Riding the Waves of Change at Work

High Performance Goal Setting
Using Intutition to Conceive & Achieve Your Dreams

Brain Boosters
Foods & Drugs that Make You Smarter

Drug Testing at Work
A Guide for Employers

Passing the Test
An Employee's Guide to Drug Testing

The Healing Magic of Cannabis
It's the High that Heals

Turning Around
Keys to Motivation and Productivity

Docpotter

Table of Contents

1
Know Thy Self

WE MUST KNOW OURSELVES—know our habits, morals, temperament, abilities, tendencies, likes and dislikes—before we can manage ourselves for excellence. Some people liken us to puppets—controlled by all kinds of internal and external factors. The better that we know ourselves the more able we are to become the puppet-master pulling the puppet's strings.

What your heart desires is what you love and are passionate about. What is done with passion is done with ease. When propelled by passion, you easily put your best foot forward, without feeling pressured or over-worked. Rather than being deterrents, roadblocks motivate you to stretch yourself and to rise to the challenges.

He who knows man is clever; He who knows himself has insight. He who conquers men has force; He who conquers himself is truly strong."

—Lao Tzu

What Turns You On?

WHAT IS YOUR PASSION? Dig deep within yourself to find that one thing or collection of things that makes you happy. Look beyond pleasures and feel-good activities and dig for what makes your soul

Let yourself be silently drawn by the stronger pull of what you really love.

— Rumi

sing with satisfaction and pleasure. What activity or "work" is absolutely essential, without which you can't imagine living. Therein lies your passion.

What activities do you love doing? Think of several and write them down in your journal. You can use these loved activities to discover and explore your passions, to dig below the surface.

About the first activity on your list of things you love doing, ask yourself, "What do I love about this?" "What about this really matters to me?" Don't try to force an answer. Instead, quiet your mind and allow your intuition to speak to you. Be receptive and notice what thoughts occur and what images come to mind. When an image comes to mind, ask of it, "What do I love about this?" "What about this really matters to me?" Continue asking, "What do I love about this?" of the thoughts and images that come until you feel you've found what is most meaningful about the activity. Jot down notes in your journal next to the activity. Then repeat the digging process with the next activity on your list of things you love doing. Continue in this fashion with each activity you love.

This "data" that you've collected on yourself is vitally important because it points to your passions. What do these images and thoughts have in common? The common threads reveal your passions. When you work in your "passion zone' your heart sings. You can easily push through the necessary details, difficulties and routines that come with any activity. Work doesn't feel like work. Heart work, as it is sometimes called, is fulfilling and you can hardly drag yourself away from it.

Action List

Administer	Handle	Predict
Act	Heal	Prepare
Analyze	Help	Produce
Arrange	Hunt	Program
Build	Identify	Protect
Challenge	Illustrate	Publicize
Change	Improvise	Raise
Check	Increase	Recruit
Coach	Inspect	Regulate
Communicate	Inspire	Resolve
Conserve	Interview	Restore
Convince	Invent	Save
Counsel	Investigate	Secure
Create	Judge	Shape
Develop	Learn	Sort
Decide	Manage	Start
Deliver	Measure	Sue
Dominate	Mediate	Supply
Earn	Monitor	Teach
Educate	Motivate	Test
Eliminate	Negotiate	Trade
Employ	Nurture	Translate
Foster	Observe	Update
Furnish	Open	Verify
Gather	Organize	Weight
Grow	Oversee	Write
Guide	Persuade	

Identify Core Actions

RETURN TO THE LIST OF ACTIVITIES you love doing and again consider them one-at-a-time. About
each activity, ask: "What actions are involved in
this activity?" Think in terms of action verbs like:
build, create, invent, communicate, cultivate, nur-
ture, restore, heal, and so forth.

Circle the action words on the Action List
on the previous page. Add words to the list as
needed. After you have worked through all of the
activities you love doing, read the action-words
you have circled and notice how you feel when
contemplating each action. Underline or highlight
the action word you like the most. You can change
your mind later, but pick one for now. You must
start somewhere.

What Do You Value?

WHAT IDEALS DO YOU FEEL STRONGLY ABOUT? What
do you stand for. Every time you make a choice
about doing one thing as opposed to another, you
make a value decision. When you have a decision
that involves two or more conflicting values that
are of major importance to you, the decision can
be extremely difficult to make. You can, however,
make these decisions more effectively if you have
some idea of what your most important values are
and the priority that you give to each.

For your work to be satisfying, it must be
compatible with your values. For some people,
money, power, prestige, and status are what it
takes for a job to be rewarding. Others must
experience meaning or purpose in the work itself

for a job to be satisfying. The following exercises contain lists of work and personal values that could form the basis of your career-planning decisions.

On the Values List below check those values that are important to you. Contemplate for a few seconds each value checked, noticing how you feel when doing so. Then, from those values checked, circle the three values that are most important to you. Finally choose from the three values you circles as being important, chose one value to serve as your guiding principle.

Values List

Achievement	Friendship	Pleasure
Awareness	Generosity	Power
Balance	Happiness	Reason
Beauty	Health	Rebellion
Caution	Honesty	Recognition
Comfort	Humility	Respect
Competence	Humor	Salvation
Control	Independence	Security
Creativity	Individuality	Serenity
Discipline	Insight	Service
Duty	Integrity	Sex
Equality	Intelligence	Simplicity
Excellence	Justice	Spirituality
Excitment	Learning	Spontaneity
Expression	Love	Stimulation
Fairness	Modesty	Tolerance
Faith Family	Nature	Trust
Fitness	Openness	Wealth
Freedom	Order	Wisdom
Friendly	Peace	Work

2

Get Started

GETTING STARTED IS AN ISSUE with any project. People who are excellent self-managers self-start. They get themselves going without being prodded and work without a boss looking over their shoulder, which means that they can work independently. This is not to say that poor self-managers cannot work without a boss standing over them. They can, but do so by standing over themselves making unreasonable demands on themselves, which they enforce with criticism and threats.

You don't have to be hard on yourself to accomplish a lot and perform excellently. Whatever you set out to do, you must get started to accomplish it. This is where a lot of people get stuck. Beginning something new, especially when it is related to "work" can trigger resistance.

Beginning is Heroic

SWEDISH PHILOSOPHER Kierkegaard observed that we judge heros, such as Charles Lindbergh, by their results—record-breaking solo flight across the Atlantic. Yet, the actual heroic act was in making a beginning—in starting in the face of uncertainty. Why? Because when starting the hero doesn't know how things will turn out.

Beginning always meets with resistance because inertia must be broken and because of the uncertainty of the outcome. In the beginning the risks are plentiful and the rewards few. Just because you start, doesn't mean that you will succeed. If you do succeed, rewards may be months, years, even decades in the future. One thing is for sure, however. You will never succeed at anything unless you get started.

People judge a person's greatness by the result of his actions. If the man who has to act tries to judge himself by the result, he will never begin And even if the result overwhelms the world with joy, it cannot help the hero; for he has no knowledge of the result until the whole thing is accomplished and it is not in this that he became a hero, but through the fact that he made a beginning.

—Kierkegaard

Break Your Inertia

THINKING BACK TO HIGH SCHOOL PHYSICS, you may recall Newton's principles of inertia, which state that a body at rest will tend to stay at rest and a body in motion will tend to stay in motion. Before you begin something you are a body at rest—in a state of inertia. It requires a tremendous effort to overcome the inertia of a large rock to get it to roll; but once the rock moves it takes less effort to keep the it rolling.

The same is true for you. Once you get started, it's easier to keep moving. Before you start on any project, large or small, you are a body at rest. To get started, you must move that rock—get

Before you begin something you are a body at rest—in a state of inertia. your body into motion. This can be particularly challenging when the activity is something you don't want to do. However, don't be fooled. Even when the activity is something you want to do, you can experience resistance to starting. To get started you must break your inertia to get into motion.

Most work projects are not accomplished in one sitting, but stretch out over weeks, months, even years. Nonetheless the inertia metaphor holds. Working toward a goal requires a large effort in the beginning to overcome inertia to get yourself moving. This is most evident in procrastinators who just cannot seem to get started.

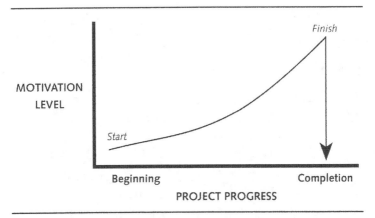

In the chart above you can see that at the beginning of a project motivation is low and builds as the project increases, with the peak of motivation being just before completion. At completion, motivation generally drops off. This cycle holds for working at one sitting or for projects that stretch over time.

Take Small Steps

THE EASIEST WAY TO GET YOURSELF INTO MOTION is by taking a small step, one that requires you to move only a short distance or to do something small—something you can easily do. Make a list. Call someone. Completing the step sets you into motion and breaks your inertia. You've started. Then take another *small* step.

The laws of inertia state that a body in motion will tend to say in motion. Suppose your car stalls and you want to push it a distance to get it off the road. When at a standstill it can take two people making a considerable effort to get the car rolling. Whereas, once rolling, keeping the car rolling requires much less effort because objects in motion will tend to keep moving.

You can keep yourself in motion with small steps. Accomplishing the first step brings a feeling of success. Success begets success. Good self-managers set themselves up to succeed by demanding only very small steps—just enough to keep in motion.

Poor self-managers sabotage themselves by demanding too much for one step. Then berate themselves when they fail to meet their unreasonable demands. Avoid this macho approach of demanding huge steps, forcing you to strain through

difficulty. Not only is the large step approach painful, it is a setup to fail. Don't put obstacles in your path.

Build a gradual ramp that you can move up easily. We climb the mountain small step by small step. The surest way to reach a goal is to break it into achievable small steps.

Instruct Yourself

OUR MINDS ARE CONTINUALLY FILLED with images and words, sometimes called a stream of consciousness. Even though it may seem to come from someone or someplace else, this never-ending monologue is you talking to yourself and the primary way that you manage yourself.

In a sense you are both you and your boss. You can refine the methods of this internal boss by *purposefully* instructing yourself. For one thing, it helps you to keep focused on the objective at hand and to block out distracting thoughts.

If you were managing an employee getting started on the project at hand, what would you say? How would you instruct that person? For example, you might say, "You don't have to do a lot today, just get started. Begin by listing several things that you can do right now to begin."

Of course, you are talking to yourself constantly. With instructing yourself the key is doing so purposefully—on purpose. Simply talk yourself through what you are doing. By so doing you take command of yourself to become a better self-manager.

Keep Beginning

ALWAYS FOCUS ON MAKING A BEGINNING. Each time you sit down to work, it is a beginning. Switching from one project to another is a beginning. If you keep "beginning"—regardless of how far into something you are—you will eventually get to the finish. When I hike up a mountain, I don't focus on the summit; instead I look to the switch-back ahead. When I reach it, I look to the next switch-back.

Expect to get distracted, to get side-tracked, derailed. Expect to lose momentum. Expect to procrastinate. You're human.

This book that you have in your hands is the result of thousands of beginnings and thousands of small steps. I begin a chapter by making an outline of topics to be covered. I begin a topic by writing two sentences. Phone rings—momentum is lost. I begin again.

There will be times when you lose momentum. Projects get set aside for many reasons. There may be a crisis. You may go on vacation or have to attend to other priorities. You may run into an obstacle or some internal resistance. You are human and not perpetual motion machine.

Expect to get distracted, to get side-tracked, derailed. Expect to lose momentum. Expect to procrastinate. You're human. Don't criticize yourself, which doesn't help. Instead, begin again—and again and again and again.

Often your momentum will slow or plateau because a step is too large or too difficult. When this happens, divide the step into smaller steps to get yourself going again. No step is too small. Always think: How can I get moving? What one small thing can I do right now to get started? Then do it!

Set Yourself Up to Succeed

EXCELLENT SELF-MANAGERS set themselves up to succeed. When playing volley ball we "set up" a team member to score by tapping the ball in front of them so that they have a perfect shot. Set yourself up so that it is easy for you to succeed.

By using small steps you set yourself up to succeed because working through the steps is easy, you can hardly fail. Demanding of yourself output that you *know* you can accomplish is setting yourself up to succeed.

Poor self-managers sabotague themselves by demanding output that is overly ambitious, While they may achieve 90% of what they demanded of themselves, they failed to achieve what they demanded. Better to demand a smaller output, achieve it and then raise the mark, achieve that and raise the mark again. This creates success momentum.

Excellent self-managers under-promise. They promise a lesser output and then produce more than promised. They under-promise and over-deliver. Recipients are delighted, so excellent self-managers are perceived as producers. By contrast poor self-managers over-promise, which they rarely deliver. So even when they actually do deliver a lot, when it is less than promised, they have failed and are criticized.

3
Keep Moving

ONCE YOU HAVE GOTTEN YOURSELF INTO MOTION, you must keep yourself moving to get where you want to go. This means managing your motivation, which is a kind of internal engine that moves you.

There are two ways to move: *toward something* or *away from* something. Moving toward or "seeking motivation" is at play when you act to get something positive. Making a final edit of a report so that the Division Chief will be impressed with your extra effort is an example. Here the drive was seeking recognition and appreciation.

Moving away or "avoidance motivation" is operating when a negative situation exists and you act to avoid it or to turn the negative off. Suppose you have a headache, for example. You take an aspirin to turn off the headache.

A person who pretends to look busy when the boss walks by is engaging in avoidance motivation. The pretender hopes to avoid being given more work. Another example is making a final edit of a report because you're afraid that the Division Chief will criticize your spelling again.

Kinds of Motivation	
SEEKING	**AVOIDING**
Moving Toward a positive	Moving Away from a negative
Going with the Flow	Swimming upstream

You Move You

HOW DO YOU MOTIVATE YOURSELF? By striving for positives? Or by avoiding negatives? Clearly, moving to gain positives—seeking motivation—is the way to go? Yet, we are frequently motivated by negatives—by fears and anxieties—that we work to avoid or turn off. We do things so that we will *not* get more work, *not* fail the test, *not* be laughed at, *not* get a speeding ticket or to *turn off* criticism, stress, and other negatives.

Unwittingly, we often create negative situations to avoid in order to get ourselves moving. Avoidance motivation *requires a threat to avoid* to get moving—without it you can't get going. When you berate yourself with fears of low performance reviews to get started, you are using fear and avoidance to get yourself moving.

Don't be mistaken, when employing avoidance motivation, you can get things done, but it means working under a threat, which creates anxiety and resistance. Worse, you can get stuck in avoidance motivation so that you cannot get started unless a threat is loom-

Motivation is what gets you started. Habit is what keeps you going.

—Jim Ryan

We often create negative situations to avoid in order to get ourselves moving. ing. Work can become a vicious cycle of procrastination and threats. This reflects a predominate view of work as a necessary evil, something we do because we must and that we would quit immediately upon winning the lottery. This is the dilemma of the poor self-manager.

Excellent self-managers get things done without so much struggle. When you focus on positives you want to achieve you are seeking a positive to get moving. Seeking motivation promotes self-starting—and finishing.

It is easy to fall into a habitual pattern of moving only to avoid negatives. Avoidance motivation is learned early on from parents and in schools. Many of us endured long, boring lectures where we pretended to be interested in order to avoid incurring the wrath of teachers. In college many of us developed a habit of procrastinating when it came to studying, then cramming to avoid failing grades.

Acknowledge Yourself

IS THE GLASS HALF-FULL OR HALF-EMPTY? Excellent self-managers focus on half-fullness—on what they are doing that is working—however small. Positive attention provides the encouragement necessary to keep making small steps. Poor self-managers do just the opposite. They focus on their failures and criticize what they have done poorly. Self-criticism tends to set up a vicious cycle of avoidance, whereas self-acknowledgment promotes seeking motivation—and self-confidence.

Notice the ways you have performed well, including small ways, then acknowledge this progress to yourself. Yes, actually tell yourself silently, or aloud, what you have done well. Say favorable things to yourself about your performance. Additionally, tell others how you've performed well.

Diligence is the mother of good luck and God gives all things to industry. Work while it is called today, for you know not how much you may be hindered tomorrow. One today is worth two tomorrows; never leave off till tomorrow that which you can do today.

—Benjamin Franklin

Self-acknowledgement is important when starting—particularly when starting is difficult. Talk to yourself the way that a coach or personal trainer would. If you're not a sports buff or never had a trainer, then talk to yourself as a good friend would. When managing yourself you are functioning like a personal trainer or coach. Don't wait for a perfect outcome. Notice progress—even if it is small. Then comment positively to yourself about it. Ignore what you haven't done and focus on what you have done.

Ability to self-reward increases personal power because you are less dependent on others for acknowledgement. Autonomy and confidence increases as you master moving yourself up small steps by stroking yourself. Notice and comment positively to yourself about what you have done, about how you are moving towards where you want to be. "Good, that was faster than last time." "Hum mm, yes. That's it."

Hold Out Your Own Carrot

YOU CAN GET A MULE TO MOVE by threatening it with a stick; or you can hold out a carrot to entice the mule forward. Excellent self-managers hold out carrots in front of themselves.

Arrange what you do so that you are *working for* a reward that you give yourself when you achieve the mark you set. While it seems easy, implementing this simple strategy often goes a rye. Good intentions aside, you skip the work and go right for the reward. You keep watching TV (reward) and don't do the bills (work), for example.

Sometimes we structure our work in self-defeating ways. Consider Richard, a contractor. Richard's bids for remodeling, for new and repeat customers alike, include a large up-front payment, followed by installment payments when certain steps are completed. With the bid accepted and that first big check in his pocket, Richard always felt terrific. But his good feelings never lasted.

Richard's customers were constantly disgruntled, not by his workmanship, but by his work style. Richard has a large family and was financial at the edge so the advanced payment ran out fast. He had to set aside remodeling jobs to do handyman jobs. So remodeling dragged along. Not surprisingly, Richard got to hating to go to the job site. .

Richard is a poor self-manager. He inches along. His customers got angry with him because of the delays. His wife got angry because he doesn't bring home enough money. Life and work was quiet desperation for Richard.

Let's analyze how Richard structured his reward schedule. As soon as a bid was accepted Richard received a large check, which was definitely rewarding. But what had been rewarded? What did Richard do to get the money? He wrote up a bid for remodeling and had it accepted. Bidwriting, not remodeling was rewarded.

Because money was tight, Richard and his wife immediately spent the advanced payment. Richard had do a considerable amount of work before he got another payment installment. Effectively Richard had to work for two or three weeks, or more, without any pay—which was definitely not rewarding, especially when bills were piling up at home. In fact, psychologically it was punishing. Punishment sabotages motivation.

Richard had to do handyman projects to get some cash, which meant leaving the project for which he had been paid in advance. Richard got money when he left, so was rewarded for leaving the project he'd been paid to do, rather than for working on the remodel.

Not too surprisingly, customers got increasingly annoyed by lack of progress and criticized Richard. Being criticized is punitive. Under all of this pressure, Richard procrastinated, got to the job site late in the morning—on the days he actually showed up—and left early, which further agonized his customers. Richard's work was a vicious cycle of negativity and punishment. He pushed himself through it because he had looming bills at home.

Richard is the poster child of a poor self-manager—even though he has the ability to do quality work and actually does work hard when he is finally at the job site.

Restructure

RICHARD'S WORK WAS STRUCTURED around working to avoid, which made working a misery. He needed to rework his work and payment structure.

Richard dropped the large up-front payment. Richard didn't employ any helpers and the customer paid for the materials, so Richard did not have any payroll or budget. As before, the bid had scheduled installments as the project progressed to certain benchmarks. However, in this new arrangement, Richard got paid *after* working and producing certain results, rather than before starting. Now Richard was getting money after performing, which was rewarding. Richard progressively increased the size of the installment payments, so that as he worked through the project his payments got larger, whereas before the installments were successfully smaller. His response to the increasing size of the pay was to work faster and longer.

With this simple change Richard became motivated as he easily moved through the work. He didn't have to leave the project for other jobs because he was getting paid regularly after performing. Working felt good and he got the job done sooner. Richard discovered that under the new structure he did more projects and made more money. Richard's customers were happier, stopped complaining and began applauding.

By changing his bidding process, Richard became more productive, had happier customers and enjoyed his work much more.

Reward Yourself

WE ALL KNOW THAT WE GET MORE WORK out of
someone when we reward them. The same holds
for ourselves. Only we often withhold treats or we
give them to ourselves "uncontingently". Contingent means "based upon". When you give yourself
treats without demanding a small step, you waste
the power of the reward—and you sabotage your
motivation.

Excellent self-managers
are generous with themselves.
They just demand "a little bit",
a small step, then "reward"
themselves with something they
want. When getting treats is
contingent upon performance
rather than giving yourself the
treat before performing, you
harness the power of seeking
motivation.

Want List

THE STRATEGY IS TO GIVE YOURSELF just about
everything you want—contingently. Do a little bit
and then give yourself a reward that you want.
To begin, you must come up with a list what you
want—big and small.

Make sure that you include things that you
routinely give yourself so that you can use the
power of these treats to motivate yourself. For
example, you may give yourself a cup of coffee, a
call to a friend, doing a crossword puzzle, going
on-line posting. These are pretty small things and

often aid procrastinate. They can be transformed into powerful motivators simply by requiring some small performance *before* giving yourself the treat.

Add medium-sized and big things to your Want List. These might include a weekend mini-vacation, a new outfit, DVDs to watch in your home theatre. Earning these pleasures should require several small steps—reaching a benchmark.

Finally your Want List should include big ticker rewards, like a new car, cruse to an exotic port, a vacation home. Achieving a significant goal earns one of these big re-wards. Of course, you move yourself towards the big re-wards with lots of little "car-rots" from your Want List that you hold out to yourself.

Reward Work with Work

WHEN REWARDS ARE GIVEN CONTINGENTLY—earned for completing a particular task—they serve as a reinforcement. While we think of a reward as something positive and desirable, the technical definition of "reinforcement" is "a consequence that makes a behavior more likely". So something becomes a reinforcer or reward by virtue of its impact upon performance—not by anything inher-ent in the reward itself.

As it turns out certain work activities can be used to reinforce other work. Which work? Rather than thinking of pleasurable activities, look for frequency. When there is nothing pressing, what are you likely to do? Make phone calls? Straighten up and file papers? Read trade journals?

Activities that you are most likely to do are called "high probability behaviors"; whereas activities you are least likely to do are called "low probability behaviors". Research has shown that high probability behaviors can function as reinforcers. What this means is that if you do a little work you tend to put off and then follow it with a little work you tend to do right away, you will be more motivated and get more done.

Excellent self-managers don't badger themselves to get things done. Instead they arrange their work to be more motivating—like doing a little work that they like doing less and then rewarding themselves with a little work that they do frequently or that they like doing more.

Avoid Perfectionism

PERFECTIONISTS' DEMAND NOTHING LESS than perfect performance. Doomed to always fall short, they use guilt and other punitive techniques to coerce themselves into performing—to avoid their own wrath. Perfectionists spend their lives caught in a vicious cycle of procrastination and self-flagellation.

Cognitive psychologists consider perfectionism to be a "thinking disorder" because perfectionists create so much self-distress by the impossible standards they set for themselves.

Perfectionists are among the poorest self-managers—and the most miserable. Contrary to popular opinion, perfectionists are not superior performers. In fact, overall their track record often falls short. The problem is that perfectionists set unrealistic criteria for success—nothing less than 99.999% is acceptable.

Realists set high, but realistic, standards and focus on what they do well, to provide a steady stream of self-acknowledgement that fuels motivation, leading to more success. Ninety percent is an "A", after all. Perfectionists often regale against this as being not good enough. However, if you do everything at 90%—or 85%, which is a "B+"—or even 80%, for that matter—you are doing very well, indeed! When you set your criteria at realistic levels, you get more done, achieve more success, and enjoy yourself more.

Suppose both a perfectionist and a realist are preparing a customer presentation. Who is likely to complete their presentation first? Probably the realist who sets an achievable standard. While the perfectionist labors away on refinement after refinement, the realist goes on to prepare and give the presentation to a second, perhaps a third customer.

Because perfectionists set unrealistically stringent standards, they continually experience failure. Realists, in contrast, win more often. Perfectionists tend to self-criticize, because they consider anything less than perfect as inadequate. Since perfect is unattainable, they can never be adequate. Excellent self-managers—realists, on the other hand, make realistic demands upon themselves, and applaud what they do well—which is most of what they do.

4

I Think So I Am

We continually create our lives with what we think about. Our thoughts interpret information from the senses, set our expectations, and frame our vision. We know ourselves only because the brain tells us who we are—it transfers signals from the world, signals from the body and signals from our thoughts and imaginations

Cat scans of working brains have shown that thoughts and memories record a "neurosignature." The more we think a particular thought or recall a memory, the more indelible becomes the signature, sort of like a finger print. Of course, how it happens exactly is not fully understood, but we can say that the way you think changes your brain circuits, which changes you.

> "Cogito, ergo sum."
> "I think, therefore I am.."
> —René Descartes

Like a computer, your brain is both hard-wired and soft-wired. Functions that are built into the system are hard-wired. Instincts, for example, are hard-wired including the will to live, fear of heights and snakes. Learned pathways, are soft-wired and unique to the individual.

Soft-wiring is created by repetitive thoughts, which causes impulses to continually retrace certain neural paths—until following that circuit becomes virtually automatic, locking you into patterns of thinking and behaving. It's a form of conditioning—programming—leading to your acting in habitual ways without awareness in most cases. Soft-wiring is a circular thing where emotions and personality influence biology—literally building neural pathways in the brain, and biology, in turn, influences emotion. Consequently, there is tremendous potential for negative vicious cycles to set into motion.

Metaphorically we are biochemical robots run by a computer that can be programmed and that can program itself. The computer on your desk is programmed with a "language"—DOS, Java, Unix—which is a string of words and symbols. Similarly, we program our biocomputer with words and images.

You program and re-program yourself by constantly talkng to yourself.

We are metaprogrammers constantly programming our biocomputers. We do this by talking to ourselves. The constant monologue in your mind is you talking to you. What psychologists call "self-talk". In some cases, what you learn to tell yourself comes from your parents. Your mother taught you that you would always fail. Without realizing it, you learned to tell yourself that you will always fail, as an example. "You'll screw up," you tell yourself. And guess what, you do!

You have a style of talking to yourself—of self-programming. Commonly we blame others—"You

made me . . . !" Or tell ourselves that another
person "should" have done something-or-the-other,
like call if they will be late", and when they don't
that it is an "awful" offense, for example.

David Burns identified several common types of
distorted thinking in *Feeling Good: The New Mood
Therapy*. These include all-or-nothing (always/nev-
er), generalizing, selective perception, negativity,
jumping to conclusions, magnification or minimiza-
tion, emotional reasoning, rigid demands, labeling,
blame, and 20/20 hindsight. Continuing with the
metaphor, when we program ourselves with such
distorted thinking, we program in "bugs", "worms"
and "viruses" causing performance problems.

It *feels* as if the thoughts occur independent
from you. Not so. You are the one talking to
yourself.

Plasticity

THE ENCOURAGING THING is that the brain has tremendous capacity for change or what psychologists call "plasticity". Soft-wiring is malleable
because it is learned. It is adaptable. We can
reprogram our brains.

When you change the way you think, your
picture of the world changes, the way you act
and feel changes—your life changes. Sound like
a dramatic claim? The fact is you feel the way
you think. Negative feelings like anxiety, depression, and anger don't actually result from the bad
things that happen, they result from the way you
think about those negative events

Automatic Self-Talk

MOST OF US EXPERIENCE THINKING as a sort of silent talk—a seemingly spontaneous monologue going on in our minds. Usually we don't notice our self-talk because it goes on automatically. We react without being aware that we are reacting to something we told ourselves about the situation. This is called "automatic thoughts". These thoughts are often a short-hand, with one or two words conveying the entire meaning about a situation. Following the previous example, you might tell yourself, "Always failing!" Or when a co-worker you don't like comes to mind, you tell yourself, "Such a jerk!" Automatic thoughts can be and often are irrational. What you tell yourself can be contrary to factual evidence, as well as over-generalized, absolutistic, one-sided and dogmatic.

Yet, self-talk sounds like the truth to you inside your mind, talking to yourself. So thoughts driven by expectations and by prejudices go unchallenged. You accept things that you say to yourself that you would never accept if someone else said them, because they occur so quickly that it's hard to question the validity of a belief when you're hardly aware of it.

The thing is, this self-talk controls your life, shaping you, limiting your options, controlling you—programming you. Since you are the one talking to yourself, you control yourself by talking to yourself, yet you don't control what you say because the thoughts are learned—conditioned, programmed, automatic. You continually re-program yourself.

Don't believe everything you tell yourself.

We talk to ourselves almost every waking moment and much of the time when we're asleep.

Self-Talks Is Persuasive

WE ARE, after all, thinking creatures. We solve problems, we dream dreams and pour out our souls in poetry. Humans carry on a constant internal monologue. We talk to ourselves almost every waking moment and much of the time when we're asleep. We tell ourselves what to do, what to think, what to believe and what to feel. And most of the time we don't even notice ourselves doing this.

We tend to think that thoughts are some sort of ethereal process that go on outside our control. But actually thoughts are behaviors—internal behaviors. Behaviors that go on inside and that only you can observe. Thinking is something you do—a habit. Habits are automatic behaviors. We all have some bad thinking habits; poor self-managers have a lot of bad thinking habits. You were not born with predisposition to anxious self-talk—or angry self-talk, or guilty self-talk, or depreciating self-talk. You learned it! Just as you can change bad behavioral habits, you can change bad thinking habits.

Listen With EARs

ONE WAY TO UNDERSTAND how thinking influences feeling is with something I call, "EARs", which stands for E-event, A-appraisal, R-response. Use EARs to hear what you say to yourself.

EARs

E = Event

A = Appraisal

R = Response

Here's how it works. An event takes place, like co-worker taking credit for your work. You respond—you get angry. It *feels like* the co-worker's dishonesty *made you* angry, but it didn't. *What made you angry is what you told yourself about what the co-worker did.* At point A, the appraisal, you told yourself something about the event, like "George cheated me!" and your body responded to what you said—your appraisal: "I've been cheated"—about the event.

The factor that "causes" you to respond occurs between the event and the response. During that instant you make a judgment about the event: Is this good or is it bad? Friend or foe? Safe or unsafe? If you tell yourself, "This person has wronged me" when someone takes credit for your work you will probably feel quite angry. But being wronged is not the only way to view the event. For example, you could think, "This always happens to me. No matter how hard I work, I always lose;" then you would probably feel discouraged and depressed. Alternatively, you could tell yourself, "There's been a mistake. I can correct it." Here, you would feel more hopeful.

Events are just events. An event in and of itself doesn't cause you to respond, except for something physical, like burning yourself on a hot stove, for example. In this case, the event or being burned, causes pain and you to quickly pull back from the stove. It is part of your hard-wiring, a built-in instinctual response to pain.

If you observed yourself in slow motion, you would notice that it is the judgment you make about the event that triggers your emotional response. Something happens and you tell yourself, "This is awful. This shouldn't happen to me. This is a disaster," for example. Then you respond to those catastrophic thoughts, not the event. It's subjective. You're constantly judging—drawing conclusions, making appraisals and then responding to these judgments as if they were objective reality. It's hard to find something that the mind regards with complete impartiality because there is always a judgment, however mild—a liking or a disliking. Judgments happen in a fraction of a second, without realizing it. You evaluate everything as you perceive it, assigning emotional values as you do.

Judgments happen at the A step of EARs. Judgments are appraisals—conclusions that you tell yourselves about the event. "It is not good enough!" "It is a disaster!" "I'm at risk!" You respond to your judgmental thoughts, not to the event. The event does not cause your angry feelings. It's your judgments about events in your life that trigger disappointment, fear, anxiety, anger and other emotions.

Even though there are a multitude of possible responses to an event, you don't stop to consider alternative views because you have a habitual way of responding to particular events, which feels "natural." You don't question your instantaneous judgments because you believe that your view is the one "real" view. In most cases, this all goes on so quickly that you're not even aware that you are leading your life by what you are saying to yourself and not noticing what you are doing.

"Men are not disturbed by things", Epictetus, the Greek philosopher observed, "but by the views they take of them." Quite often, your view is clouded by self-defeating beliefs and expectations. What you tell yourself about things creates your mood. You get upset because of the way you think about events. How you feel depends predominately on your value judgments and self-talk not what actually happens in the world.

5

Switch Emotions

S PECIFIC KINDS OF FEELINGS result from specific kinds of thoughts. When you feel upset, the thoughts that make you feel bad are often illogical and distorted even though subjectively they may seem very real. Change the way you talk to yourself about events and you change the way you respond. When you learn to talk to yourself in a supportive **Change the way you talk to yourself about events and you change the way you respond.** and encouraging way you can change the way you feel.

You can change the way you feel by changing what you tell yourself about events. It is as simple as that. You can do it—if you set yourself out to do it. Changing how you talk to yourself is like reprogramming a computer's operating system. Afterwards the computer performs differently. With the human biocomputer it's a matter of self-programming. When you change what you say to yourself about what happens to you, like the computer, you will have changed the programming and will perform differently.

The brain is excited to a greater or lesser degree, but there are no qualities of excitement, like joy excitement or fear excitement, for example. Excitement on the brain cell level is essentially

Changing how you talk to yourself is like reprogramming a computer's operating system. the same whether it is joyful or fearful to the person. Whether excitement is joyful or fearful is determined predominantly by what you tell yourself about the sensations that you are experiencing and not by some qualitative difference in physical sensations of excitement. This is an important point because within it lies a secret of modulating your mood.

If you redefine your physical sensations—tell yourself something different from what you usually tell yourself about the sensations—your mood will change. In fact, your level of self-confidence may shift dramatically. For example, you could notice a knot in your stomach and tell yourself, "Oh, I'm really anxious about this. Everyone is looking at me and I might fail. This is terrifying. I can't take this." You can see where this is going. You can change this scenario by simply changing what you tell yourself about the sensations. You could tell yourself, "Oh, I'm very excited. This is really thrilling. Wow, look at what I'm doing. This is so exciting that I can hardly contain myself." In this second scenario you will feel more confident and have more fun.

Emotions as Switches

IN *Creating Your Ultimate Destiny*, Robert Stuberg shared his insight that when we strive for something, we are seeking to experience the emotions that we believe achieving the goal will bring. We seek joy, love, happiness, power, fulfillment, control, security and we do so by pursuing relationships, accumulating things, earning rewards and acclaim. In saving up to purchase a "muscle" car, you may be seeking the *thrill* of driving, the *envy* of friends, or the *pride* of ownership. In working towards a raise, as another example, it is not the increased money per se that you seek, but feelings of achievement, of being respected, of the fun you anticipate having when spending the extra money. Alternatively, in a down economy seeking a raise may trigger feelings of security and comfort.

Emotions are switches you can flip. Within a few seconds you can feel depressed or anxious by merely recalling a distressing situation from the past because the recollection flips the switch. By recalling and reliving a joyful time from the past, you can turn on feelings of joy. It is through our switch-flipping ability that we can read a romance novel and experience some of the giddiness that comes with a new romance.

While we all have the ability to turn various emotions on and off, most of us tend to make experiencing certain positive emotions, like pride and satisfaction, contingent upon some achievement, like getting a promotion or letter of accommodation, and withhold experiencing these emotions until we reach that marker. Obviously, even the most successful among us gets only a few promotions and letters of accommodation a year

A man who is master of himself can end a sorrow as easily as he can invent a pleasure. I don't want to be at the mercy of my emotions. I want to use them, to enjoy them, and to dominate them.

—Oscar Wilde

(if at all), which means on that schedule we rarely get to feel pride and satisfaction. As a result we spend much of our lives being frustrated and deprived of what we want. When you learn to better manage yourself, you can purposefully flip mental switches to experience the emotions you desire.

Flip Emotional Switches

LEARNING HOW TO FLIP emotional switches is a little like learning to wiggle your ears. The first step is to catch your ears moving, which often happens when speaking or laughing. The second step is to study how it feels to wiggling your ears and where it feels to identify the muscles that control your ears. As you find the muscles you gain control over ear-moving.

The ear-wiggling analogy can assist in identifying the feeling of emotions you want to experience more. You must create the feeling you want to experience, such as joy, and then study how and where joy feels. One way to create a feeling is though calling up a memory of a time when you experienced the desired emotion, such as joy, and then studying how and where joy feels.

Curiously, we are more prone to remembering negative or downer emotions than positive, uplifting ones. We all have had times when we have recalled an unpleasant situation, such as someone treating us poorly. and quickly felt the same depressing feelings as those we experienced in the actual situation. Yet, we resist doing this same process with positive recollections. We tend to accept negative memories as evidence of "truth" and what is "real", while withholding positive emotions until we are worthy, such as by getting a promotion, or achieving some other marker.

To be a good self-manager, you must break free of the notion that managing yourself requires being punitive, restrictive, withholding. When you can purposeful experience positive and reaffirming emotions, you gain tremendous control over yourself. Instead of striving for months, even years, for a raise in order to gain a sense of security—and pride, you can experience those emotions now and use them to motivate your progress along the path to getting a raise. This is what Stuberg calls "going from achieving to be happy to happily achieving."

When you can purposeful experience positive and reaffirming emotions, you gain tremendous control over yourself.

Learning to Wiggle Your Emotional Ears

BRING TO MIND A TIME when you felt amused. Review that time in your mind to familiarize yourself with the feelings of amusement. Now close your eyes and project yourself back into that moment of amusement. Notice how being amused feels. Study the sensations—where and how they feel.

Bring yourself back to the present moment, here and now. Say this affirmation to yourself: "Right now I feel so much amusement" and as you do, switch to the amusing sensation. Experience the amusing feelings, study their sensations, where and how they feel, then do what you can in your mind and body to enhance the feeling of amusement.

Repeat this exercise with other emotions like joy, love, security. Practice recalling and experiencing emotions often. One good time to practice is when in commute traffic or waiting on hold or when standing in line. The more you practice the more control you will gain to flip emotional switches when you choose.

6

Coach Yourself

WE TALK TO OURSELVES almost every waking moment and much of the time when we're asleep. We tell ourselves what to do, what to think, what to believe, what to feel. And most of the time we don't even notice ourselves doing this.

This self-talk is persuasive—and often irrational. The famous psychotherapist, Karen Horney, said that most people tend to rule themselves by the "tyranny of the shoulds". We build ideal pictures of the future with shoulds—the way the world *should* be, the way others should be, and the way we should be. When things don't conform to our notion of the way it should be, our idealized castles in the sky come tumbling down. Then we tell ourselves that it awful and a catastrophe—and we believe what we say.

When you talk to yourself day in and day out you are virtually brain washing yourself, which is problematic when you talk to yourself in ways that are unhelpful. You may create things to be angry—or guilty, or worried—about when nothing at all is a miss, for example. Remember that old saying, "Don't make a mountain out of a molehill"? That's magnification, something poor self-managers routinely do as they blow things up, so they get furious and make themselves feel crazy.

Learned Behavior

MANY OF US HAVE LEARNED judgmental self-talk that assumes a world where perfection is possible—and expected! There is always a very clear "right" way of doing things, making any other way "wrong" and leading to a constant preoccupation with what is lacking, as opposed to what is present; to fault finding and blaming. Since, of course, no one is perfect, you fall short repeatedly and feel anxious about it most of the time.

People who have grown up under a "be perfect" mandate tend to scold themselves in their self-talk and to be miserly with self-praise. Their entire focus is on self-evaluation of success and failure—only their standard is so extreme that even success gets redefined as failure. It is bad enough that they judge themselves as a failure in

Perfectionists scold themselves and are miserly with self-praise.

most things, but they worry about failing, the dire consequences of failing as well as what others will think about their having failed.

Self-talk is learned from interacting with significant adults in your world—your parents, teachers, older siblings. If the influential people in your early life were harsh, critical or judgmental, you have probably incorporated these characteristics in your self-talk. Perfectionists demand unachievable standards and then mercilessly whip themselves for small errors.

You would never consider talking to another person, especially not to someone you care about, with the same harshness that you use when talking to yourself. If you were talking to another person—to a friend, for example—you would be supportive, pointing out positives and playing down negatives. If you were talking to a friend, you would be reassuring, and challenge the severity of your criticism, for example. Yet, when you talk to yourself you leave out sensitivity and encouragement, and hammer away at yourself instead.

Supportive Self-Talk

TALK TO YOURSELF in a supportive way—the way a personal trainer would talk. Like learning any new language, learning the language of self-support takes time, practice and dedication. Supportive self-talk sounds simple and it's not that hard, really. The key is to imagine how a personal trainer or coach would talk to you. Then talk to yourself that way.

A Personal Trainer:

supports

distracts

challenges

permits

acknowledges

accepts

instructs

affirms

reassures

Try this out right now. Stop reading. Think of a dissatisfaction you with yourself. For this practice, pick a light-weight dissatisfaction, not something that is terribly distressing, just something that has been mildly nagging. In a notebook or journal, write your negative thought about yourself down verbatim. Write it out just the way you tell it to yourself.

Now, before going on, pause and take a deep breath and let it out slowly. Just breath in deeply and out slowly for a few minutes. When you feel relaxed, imagine that you have told this self-dissatisfaction to your personal trainer. What would your coach say to you about your critical self-analysis? If you don't have a personal trainer, imagine what a good friend would say. Write this statement down in your journal.

Go back to your imagination and ask again, "What would a personal trainer or supportive friend say about this situation?" Continue in this process with a few more critical thoughts.

Reprogram Self-Talk

A MAJOR STEP IN MANAGING YOURSELF for excellence is reprogramming your self-talk from critical-talk to coaching-talk. The challenge is two-fold. First you must come up with a new way of talking to yourself—a way that is encouraging and motivating. Second, you must stop the critical self-talk long enough to substitute the coaching-talk. The process you went through in the exercise is a way to uncover supportive statements. Once you know how to talk to yourself like a personal trainer or supportive friend, rather than like a fuss-budget constantly criticizing yourself, then you must actually talk to yourself like a coach—or good friend—would.

A Coach Acknowledges Progress

POOR SELF-MANAGERS FUSS AND OBSESS over what's wrong and what's missing. Since you can always find fault with something, no matter how good it is, there is always something for you to worry about. Constant criticism is demotivating. It beats you down, encouraging a "why bother?" attitude. This is just what poor self-managers do to themselves with their punitive self-talk.

Excellent self-managers talk friendly to themselves,; they talk to themselves the way that a personal trainer or coach would. Supportive friends and trainers build you up by acknowledging what you do right and what's working. They reward your efforts and accomplishments, which fosters optimism and positive feelings.

Talk to yourself the way a coach would. Use coaching self-talk to give yourself credit for steps you have taken in the desired direction—for what you are doing right! Avoid judging your progress or the degree of your efforts—that's depreciating self-talk. Praise your efforts and improvement. Encourage yourself with friendly or coaching talk and remind yourself that you are valued person even if don't accomplish everything you set out to do.

Treat yourself like a personal trainer or supportive friend would. If you are like many people you have a double standard—one for friends and one for yourself. The standard you exact upon yourself is harsh. Are you willing to treat yourself as you would treat your friend? Negative thoughts will pop into your head. It's a habit. When you become aware of depreciating talk, stop and ask yourself: "Would I say this to a friend?" Probably not. Remember, the secret of self-esteem and confidence is to treat yourself as a supportive friend or coach would.

A Coach Gives Permission

POOR SELF-MANAGERS often hold themselves to a strict standard, one no one could meet. Then they worry that they will fall short. Their negative self-talk goes nonstop, pointing out failings, all the things that could go wrong. It's awfully hard to work and excel when you're constantly faced with not quite making the mark, no matter how hard you work or how much you actually achieve.

Personal trainers and supportive friends, on the other hand, urge you to go easy on yourself and to set yourself up to win. They give you permission to make mistakes, to be less than perfect. They give you permission to go slowly, at your own pace. Friends believe in you and help you to believe in yourself.

When you talk to yourself in a supportive way, you follow this good example. You give yourself permission to make mistakes and to go at your own speed. You applaud

The secret of self-esteem and confidence is to treat yourself as a supportive friend would.

near hits, rather than bemoan near misses. Coaching self-talk builds confidence by communicating a belief in your abilities.

When you give yourself permission to be less than perfect by talking to yourself in a supportive way you discover a new freedom. Intellectually, you know that making mistakes is part of learning. When you give yourself permission to make errors and let go of constantly judging yourself, it begins to feel okay to make mistakes. Your coaching self-talk reminds you that a mistake is one step closer to a success. Equally important is giving yourself permission to have feelings and be human, without constantly telling ourself how you're failing and what you are doing wrong. Following are several generic permission statements.

PERMISSION STATEMENTS

It's okay to make mistakes
I can follow my own pace.
I can take my time.
I can listen to my feelings
I can please me too.
I can succeed
I can say no.
Everyone makes mistakes.
I learn from every mistake.
A mistake means I'm a step closer
    to success.
So what if. . . .
I made an effort and that's what's
    important.
It's okay to look silly.
I have a life. I make mistakes.

The paradoxical thing is that when you feel comfortable with making mistakes and can make them easily, you tend to perform optimally for your skill level, be it novice or pro.

Which of the permission statements speak to you? Which feel right? What other permission statements can you think of? If you are plagued by what behavior therapist Dr. Pamela Butler, author of *Talking to Yourself: The Language of Self-Support*, calls "stoppers", you might want to give some special attention to practicing coaching self-talk that gives permission. A stopper is depreciating self-talk that stops you in your tracks. You freeze—paralyzed.

Stoppers are doubt-causng self-talk that says "No!", "Don't!", and "Only if...". Stoppers catastrophes, telling you all the horrible, catastrophic events that might occur if you engage in a particular behavior. Stoppers exaggerate the risk factor so much you can feel paralyzed and do nothing. Key phrases that alert you to stoppers are "What if?" and "That would be awful!". These anxiety generating phrases can be neutralized by a permissive statement, like "So what if!" When you catch yourself saying, "What if" stop and say, "So what if" and you'll be amazed how helpful this simple change in wording can be in soothing you.

At the core of giving permission is recognizing you are the ultimate authority on you. You know how you feel better than anyone else. You know what's good for you and you hold your best interest foremost.

7

The Power of Purpose

ONE OF THE WORST THINGS that you can do is to stay for years in a line of work that you do not enjoy. Some people work all week at something that they tolerate to earn a living with the hope of doing something enjoyable on the weekends. These men and women have not found their purpose. They see their jobs as a form of drudgery or a period of purgatory that pays the bills, which they must put up with in order to enjoy the rest of their lives. Because of this attitude they will seldom achieve deep happiness or success.

If you are good at setting goals and then moving yourself toward accomplishing them, you will enjoy emotions you seek and likely accomplish a lot. In effect, you are holding out your own carrot in front of yourself leading yourself on to achieve the goals that you set, as you

Outstanding people have one thing in common: an absolute sense of mission.

—Zig Ziglar

knock down goal after goal. This is a good approach, but with only a few changes you can be a much more effective self-manager.

The hardest thing to learn in life is which bridge to cross and which to burn.

—David Russell

You may set a goal, make a plan to achieve it, work hard and achieve the goal, but something is missing. We have all had this experience. When it is repetitive you can feel that life is passing you by. If you are accomplishing what you set out to do, but not enjoying yourself and wonder, "What's the point? "Why bother?" you may be lacking a purpose.

The problem with the goal after goal approach is one of direction. You bounce willy-nilly from one goal to the next, but don't seem to be "getting anywhere". After years of achieving you may take a look at all of the possessions you've accumulated, the jobs that you've advanced through, the projects that you've completed and wonder, "What's the point of all of this?"

Search for Meaning

WHAT IS MISSING is a sense of "meaning". Why bother with this? Where am I going? What am I doing with my life? Just accumulating chits? No one wants to be merely a cog in the corporate machine. If you are like most people you want to matter, to feel important. You want to accomplish something of significance, not just put in time. You want to seek a sense of "meaningfulness" and to feel that your life amounts to something.

One needs something to believe in, something for which one can have whole-hearted enthusiasm. One needs to feel that one's life has meaning, that one is needed in this world.

— Hannah Senesh

What man actually needs is not a tension-less state but rather the striving and struggling for some goal worthy of him. What he needs is not the discharge of tension at any cost, but the call of a potential meaning waiting to be fulfilled by him.

— Victor Frankl

There are two powerful tools to for creating meaning in our lives: pursuing an important purpose and following a standard of excellence.

Provides Meaning

STRIVING TOWARDS an important purpose provides meaning. It makes what may have been insignificant into something important. As Abraham Maslow, the ground-breaking psychologist showed, we all have needs that must be filled. After we satisfy physical needs for survival—shelter, food, safety—we focus on satisfying psychological needs. Maslow believed that there are universal psychological needs we seek in the pursuit of self-actualization, which include the need to love and be loved; the need to feel important, to stand out; and the need to matter, to contribute to something larger than ourselves, to do something meaningful.

A job is a series of tasks to be completed, as determined by your employer. Just completing a series of tasks can feel like you are a rat on a wheel, going around and around, not getting anywhere or doing anything worthwhile. However, as Johnny, the bagger (who you will meet in the next chapter), shows, meaning can be found anywhere when you hook your job to accomplishing an important purpose.

Meaning does not come from what you do, but from how you view that work. An classic fable about three bricklayers illustrates.

Three Bricklayers

A BISHOP WANDERED among the workers during the construction of a Gothic Cathedral. Stopping by the first man, he asked, "What are you doing?" The man answered grumpily, "I'm laying bricks!" "Bless you," the Bishop said. To the next man, the Bishop asked, "What are you doing, my son?" The man answered, "I'm constructing a wall." "Bless you," the Bishop said.

He walked on to the third man and asked, "What are you doing?" With a look of pride the man answered, "I am building a cathedral!" "Bless you," replied the Bishop.

All three bricklayers are doing the same thing—laying bricks. The difference is the way that the bricklayers think about laying bricks. The grumpy bricklayer looks at his work as nothing more than the tedious activity of laying bricks, one-after-the-other, day after day, week after week. It is a job. By contrast, the third bricklayer, who is doing the same work, sees the larger picture—the construction of magnificent cathedral that will inspire the faithful for decades, even hundreds of years. He sees his work as an important contribution to this endeavor, which fills him with pride. Bricklaying provides meaning for the third bricklayer and he finds satisfaction in his work.

Let's translate the bricklayer story into a more modern context. As a City Manager walked through the Human Resources Department, he noticed a clerk busily typing at her computer. "What are you doing?" he asked. Grumpily, the clerk answered, "I'm classifying a job!" "Good," the Manager replied. Walking over to the clerk in the next desk, the Manager asked, "What are you doing?" The clerk answered, "I'm developing an HR program for the Department." "Very good!" the Manager replied. He walked on to a third clerk and asked, "What are you doing?" With a look of pride the clerk answered, "I'm transforming my community into a 21st century City!" "Excellent!" exclaimed the Manager.

Like the grumpy bricklayer, the grumpy clerk looks at her work as doing a job—something she does to earn her paycheck. She gets little satisfaction from it. The second clerk has a larger perspective. She sees that the job she is classifying is an important part of a larger project. As a result she feels plugged in and part of a team working on a larger project. The third clerk is working towards an important purpose—helping to transform her community into a city—which provides her with meaning and fills her with pride. When it comes to finding meaning in our work, the actual work we do is less important. What matters is how we see the work we are doing. When we see our work as fulfilling an important purpose we

have a sense of meaning, that what we do matters—we are significant.

A Purpose Creates Structure

WE SPEND YEARS IN SCHOOL where all of our time
and everything we did was structured for us.
Teachers gave assignments and paced us through
material. This structure-by-others prepared us
for the old workplace where work was routine and
tasks were largely determined by the boss. But
work in today's new
workplace we so-called   *Good luck is another*
"knowledge workers",   *name for tenacity of*
—which is just about   *purpose.*
anyone who works at a
computer—increasingly   —Ralph Waldo Emerson
must structure our
own work. Creating structure involves—defining
purpose, setting goals—and then getting started.
Ability to create structure is a new must have career skill. When you can create structure you can
work independently—and creatively.

Having a purpose provides something around
which to structure your actions. Purpose provides
direction, and tells you which way to aim. With a
purpose before you, you can set goals to achieve
that purpose and small steps to accomplish the
goals. A purpose provides a marker by which to
measure progress.

As Keniche Ohmae wrote in *The Borderless
World,* "Rowing harder does not help if the boat
is headed in the wrong direction. Applying more
muscle is no solution if the course is off."

The whole world steps aside for the man who knows where he is going.

—President Clinton

A purpose tells the outcome to be achieved. When you have a purpose, instead of proceeding willy-nilly, like the will o' the wisp, you have a direction and know what you aim to achieve—at least generally. The more clearly articulated, the more power the purpose provides in "structuring" your daily life. You know what the result you are seeking, have a map for doing so, and steps for getting there—or at least potentially.

Structure creates clarity, helps you to get started and to pace yourself. As you master yourself, you will become more adept at structuring your work. You'll be increasingly able to handle free-flowing, vaguely defined projects—the creative work which requires setting long-range goals and short-term action objectives, then dividing each into small daily, even hourly steps.

Purpose Provides Sense of Control

HELPLESS FEELINGS, feeling that no matter what you do you cannot impact your circumstances squelches motivation and is the underlying cause of job burnout, which is a kind of job depression.

When we have a sense of control over what happens to us we can tolerate more problems and set backs because we feel that, while we may not be happy with circumstances, that there is something that we can do. We can act and have an impact.

Having a purpose to pursue provides a sense of control because you know where you are going and have a plan for getting there. A purpose provides a basis upon which to base decisions and a measure to evaluate progress towards achieving the purpose. It is a guide for making choices. Purpose gives you direction in your work as well as in your personal life. It is a focus for setting goals so that they lead somewhere.

Pursuing a purpose reduces uncertainty because you have a basis for making decisions in times of confusion and change. A purpose is something to hold on to like a life preserver in choppy waters. Having a clear purpose helps you to overcome fears: fear of failure, fear of success, fear of physical harm, fear of psychological pain, fear of the unknown.

Service to Others

EVERY BUSINESS EXISTS to provide a service, to fill a need. Quid pro quo. I fix your washing machine, then you pay me. Purposes that involve helping others are the most fulfilling. Every job exists to solve a problem. When you dig down, to find the need that your work is filling and the service that you—specifically, an as individual—are providing, you can find an important purpose in any work. When Johnny realized that his bagging was a service to customers—that his purpose was to serve the customer,

Service is the rent we pay to be living. It is the very purpose of life and not something you do in your spare time.

—Marian Wright Edelman

his attitude about working was transformed. He understood that how he did his job was important because the store's future and his job, as well as his co-workers' jobs, depends upon satisfied customers coming back to shop again. Johnny understood that by helping customers to feel good about shopping at his store, he was helping his co-workers, his boss, even his community—he was making an important contribution.

Serving a Purpose Brings Happiness

LIVING IN BIGGER HOUSE or driving a shiny new car may feel like happiness for the moment, but it is "feel good." It is good to feel good, but feeling good is not happiness. Happiness is not pleasure. Pleasure is enjoyment of an outside stimuli,

The purpose of life is a life of purpose.

— Robert Byrne

whereas happiness is a state of well-being, sense of joy, contentment, satisfaction. Happiness is a belief about yourself and the outside world. Pleasure requires an external stimuli for you to experience it. Happiness does not. You can be doing something you normally experience as pleasurable but not be happy! Pleasure is rooted in the external world; happiness is rooted in the way that we see the world.

Excellent self-managers do things to feel good and use the promise of feeling good as a reward. But seeking goals like buying a new car or house are not a substitute for pursuing a purpose in life. Pursuing an important purpose—one of service to others, filling needs, solving problems—brings happiness because true happiness comes from contributing to other people's lives and making a difference for someone else. Pursuing an important purpose gives a rich sense of fulfillment that goes beyond sensory satisfaction or pleasant emotions.

8

Pursue a Purpose

P URPOSE IS AN INTENTION, a reason to do something, a justification of action, but not the
action or steps. Purpose tells a desired result,
which guides action. Purpose describes one's aim;
it points the direction. While both individuals and
organizations can have a purpose, an organization's purpose or its 'raison d'être'—reason for
existence—is referred to as its mission.

When we really enjoy our work we get outside of
ourselves to become involved totally in life and work
for the pleasure of working. We may not be able to
always do work we love, we can love the work we
do. Tying work to an important purpose can transform a job into joyful work. Work that may seem
not very important, or even drudgery, can become
meaningful when it is tied to achieving an important purpose. I am reminded of a story told by Ken
Blanchard, author of *The One Minute Manager,* about
a grocery store check out bagger. You might wonder
how such simple work could be meaningful.

Johnny was a young man with Downs Syndrome
who worked as a grocery checkout bagger. After
attending an in-ser-
vice training with
his co-workers on
customer service
that stressed that

*When you align your life to
meet purpose you live on
purpose.*

— Robert Stuberg

*Do not try to change
yourself—you are
unlikely to succeed.
Work to improve the
way you perform.
And try not to take
on work you cannot
perform or will only
perform poorly.*

—Peter Drucker

the underlying purpose of every job in the store was to providing service to their customers, Johnny wondered what he could do to provide service. Then he got an idea! He would share an inspiring "Thought for the Day" with customers so that they would leave feeling good. He wanted to give it a try.

Johnny's father helped him create several inspiring Daily Thoughts, which Johnny wrote up with colored pens on file cards. The next day as he bagged groceries, he put an "Appreciation Card" into each customer's grocery bag while saying, "Thanks for shopping here. Here's an inspiring thought to show my appreciation. Have a blessed day and come back soon."

Surprised, customers smiled and thanked Johnny for the Appreciation Card. After a few days, a wonderfully curious thing happened. The line at Johnny's checkout counter was long, even when the other checkouts had no people waiting. When the store manager invited customers to go to a shorter line, customers just smiled said that they wanted to be in Johnny's line, even if it took longer, because they wanted to get the Appreciation Card for the Day. A few customers told the store owner that they had come into the store to shop when they normally would not have—"just to get Johnny's Appreciation Card".

Bagging groceries, a job that most people think is not too important, can be meaningful and contribute to the bottom line, when one is working towards a purpose—providing service—rather than merely "doing a job"—putting groceries into bags.

Identify Your Purpose

WHEN YOU WORK FOR A COMPANY, especially if it is a large one, it is easy to fall into simply doing your job—doing a series of tasks without thinking about how what you do works towards achieving an important purpose of the enterprise. Without a purpose work, especially if it is routine, can seem like a bunch of duties and details.

You Were Not Hired to Do a Job

YOU WERE NOT HIRED TO DO A "JOB"; you were hired to solve a problem. Solving that problem is your purpose—the reason you were hired. A job is a series of tasks, usually assigned and supervised by someone else—a boss. Generally, there's one way the job has been done, so the jobholder continues doing it that way. By contrast, there may be several solutions to a problem, which requires creativity to solve.

All jobs are created to solve a problem. Johnny's bagging job was created to solve the problem of gathering up customer's groceries. When customers bag, they may overload bags, which can burst when lifted; they may under-fill bags using too many bags and running up overhead costs for the store; they may crack egg or squash bread by bagging with heavy items on top; or they may slow down the check out line, causing a jam up.

The job of bagger was created to "solve" these problems.

As businesses grow problems arise. My husband and I started a mail order business selling books in our kitchen. It was pre-internet so orders came in the mail or by phone. Soon there were too many calls for us to answer and too many orders for us to process—problem. So we created a job—Mail Order Clerk—to solve the problem. Jobs are created to solve problems.

Finding your purpose encourages looking beyond repetitive tasks and routine details to see the larger picture, one where you play an important role. Take the duties of a receptionist, which is often considered to be a position of little consequence, as an example. When asked, "What is your job?" the receptionist is likely to say, "I answer the phone, schedule appointments, and tell my boss when visitors arrive."

Without a receptionist other staff must leave their work to greet, screen, and route people who call or come to the office. Clients wander into private attorney meetings; patients interrupt doctors' examinations. Customers leave in a huff because there is no one to help them. Phones ring endlessly until prospective clients go elsewhere. Receptionists are needed to solve these problems.

Importantly, the receptionist creates that critical first impression as customers enter the company. A good first impression can lead to a sale; a bad impression could turn a customer away forever. Consequently, receptionists set the stage for the sales staff. Clearly, the receptionist's actions are vitally important to the company.

Similarly, accountants, marketing directors, and CEOs all exist in the company to solve particular problems. Unfortunately, many employees as well as many employers have lost touch with this fact. When work was so specialized that a person did nothing but screw on a widget, it was difficult to see the bigger picture. Bureaucratic paper pushing often obscures the real purpose for being hired.

Look Beyond Tasks

TO DISCOVER THE PURPOSE OF YOUR JOB, analyze the problem that you were hired to solve. Be careful to not get caught up in the tasks that comprise your job. For example, consider the library clerk who re-shelves the books that patrons leave around. The clerk collects books left on the tables and counters, sequences the books in the cart according to the cards numbers, pushes the cart through the stacks, puts the books back on the shelves in their correct place, and so forth. These are tasks, not problems. To discover the purpose, the clerk must uncover the problem that he or she solves by collecting and re-shelving the books.

Envision the Problem Unsolved

IMAGINE WHAT WOULD HAPPEN if the problem you were hired to solve was left unsolved? What if no one re-shelved the books? Envision an exaggerated outcome of what would happen if the problem were ignored.

In the library, day-after-day books would pile up on tables and in carts until more books were in the piles than on the shelves. This pile up would lead to patrons being unable to find books on the shelves, since they would likely be in the piles. It would not take too many weeks before the library would be in such chaos as to be unusable and would have to close its door.

Returning to Johnny, the bagger, when imaging his problem unsolved (and exaggerated) he saw customer's bags bursting with cans and bottles rolling around in the street, with eggs breaking and bread loaves flattened after a customer puts them into the bag improperly or under something heavy, the checkout line would be backed up into the food isles. Frustrated customers would be arguing and leaving in a bad mood, promising to never return to "that rotten store."

See the Problem

CLOSE YOUR EYES AND RELAX by breathing in and out slowly and deeply. In your imagination picture a movie screen on the inside of your forehead. Ask yourself: "Why does my company employ me? Why am I here? What would happen if no one were doing my job? What would happen if no one were solving the problem I was hired to solve? What would happen if the problem that I'm here to solve were left unsolved?" The objective in asking these questions is to get a picture of the black hole, of the problem itself.

"See" the problem occurring on your mental screen. It helps to exaggerate the problem. Study what you see. How does the problem affect others? What secondary problems are caused by your problem going unsolved? Identify

The secret of success is constancy of purpose.

—Benjamin Disraeli

those spin-off problems and watch them occurring. Follow these problem-causing chains out to the end. What happens? How does the problem being left unsolved affect the overall organization? How does your problem being unsolved affect customers? Repeat this exercise several times, until you get a clear picture of the problem you were hired to solve.

Make sure you focus on the problem you were hired to solve, not the solution you've been implementing. For example, John, an association librarian, described his problem as "organizing and cataloging reports and other vital documents." Organizing and cataloging are not problems. They are actions or procedures John used to solve problems of disorganization. The problem assigned to John to solve was the chaos in which the reports and documents often were lost and the time it takes to find them. Looking beyond the immediate problem, John could see that because reports were often misplaced, association executives were not adequately briefed and lost credibility; this situation led to lost membership and declining treasury balance.

From this vantage point, John's job took on greater meaning, as he began to see that he was playing a significant part in fulfilling an important purpose of the enterprise.

Discovering Your Life's Purpose

MANY PEOPLE DON'T KNOW WHY they are living the life they lead and doing the things they do. They don't think of themselves as having a purpose. As a result, they feel lost, a drift, helpless, and at the whim of a senseless world. If you sometimes feel like you are treading water, articulating your purpose in life will give you a sense of direction and meaning.

The human spirit has a hungering for meaning. "Why" is one of the first questions a child embraces. "Why, Daddy?" "Why does the moon shine?" "Why do dogs bark?" "Why do I sleep?" "Why?" "Why?" "Why?" A life's purpose is an all-encompassing answer to the question, "Why?" It is the "reason" for your being here. It inspires and motivates you to make strides in the direction you set for yourself.

Your purpose is as unique as you are. When you get in touch with having a "purpose" you will experience a greater sense of control in your life. Looking at your daily moments through the lens of your life purpose provides inspiration—it brings spirit into your life—from which you can gather motivation. It provides a context for your dreams to come true. Hitching on to your life's purpose provides direction, helps organize your efforts and gives you something to measure your progress against. In short, you are the pilot in this adventure called "your life".

He who has a why to live can bear almost any how.

—Nietzsche

Your life's purpose is completely in your hands. No one else can determine the direction of your life, unless you turn yourself over to them.

The basic rule of thumb is to align your purpose with your needs, abilities, and desires. Focus on your strengths because you get more mileage working to your strengths more than always trying to improve your weaknesses.

Know Thyself

THE WAY YOU LIVE YOUR LIFE is an expression of your purpose, whether this purpose operates consciously or subconsciously. The reason that you get up each day reveals something about the central purpose in your life. If you get out of bed because you don't want to lose your job, then your purpose is rooted in security. If you get up because people will judge you if you don't, then you are motivated by seeking approval. If you get up to feed your kids and get them ready for school, then family is your focus.

Your needs—money, shelter, food—dictate what you must do. Your abilities—education, skills, talents, education—dictate what you can do. And your desires—working with animals, teaching children—show what you want to do. Your purpose tells you what you should do.

To discover your purpose you must know yourself—What are your passions? What motivates you? What gives you satisfaction? What are your abilities? What is your temperament?

He who knows man is clever; He who knows himself has insight. He who conquers men has force; He who conquers himself is truly strong."

—Lao Tzu

What Group Can You Serve?

YOUR LIFE PURPOSE revolves around being of service. What groups do you care strongly about? Who do you want to help? What charities do you support? These might include the homeless, disabled vets, autistic children, wolves, seniors, children of immigrants, historic houses, urban sprawl, environment, climate, and so forth.

Make a list of groups that you would like to serve. Then choose the single most important group to you, the one that you feel the strongest about. This is your target.

Put the three components together and you'll have the beginnings of your purpose in life. Start with the group you want to serve—say saving historic houses—and pair it with actions you love doing. If you love teaching, you can creating workshops about saving old buildings. If you love creating, you may develop plans for saving buildings. If you love working with your hands, you might do some renovating work yourself. Alternatively, you might restore such buildings, then rent out units in them.

You might serve your elected target as an entrepreneur, creating a business to serve them. Or you might hold a series of jobs in which you serve the group.

What is Your Legacy?

IT WOULD BE GREAT if we had a "purpose formula" in to which we could plug certain values and it yield our purpose. There are no hard and fast rules. You must work with the variables—your

values, what you love doing, who you want to service—massaging them until it rings true for you.

Another approach to the roots of your purpose
is to consider the legacy you want to leave? How
do you want to be remembered? The possibilities
are unlimited. Perhaps you want to leave a body
of helpful works, like Ben Franklin did. Perhaps
you strive to instill solid values in your children.
Perhaps you will work to save helpless animals or
develop a live-saving vaccine. Thinking about how
you want to be remembered can help you to focus
in on your purpose.

9

Set Magnetic Goals

A GOAL IS A TARGET TO SHOOT AT. It is a result toward which effort is directed. It is an outcome to be achieved. Usually a goal is a statement of what you want to achieve or where you want to go. Goals focus your efforts. They tell you where to shoot and which way to go.

Of course, we all know that we "should" set goals if we want to succeed in life and to get anywhere. But with that said, pursuing a goal can be an exercise in drudgery. You only have to force yourself through the steps, often with various threats of self-punishment for falling short a few times before you become "goal phobic". Just hearing the question; "What are your goals?" can bring on a sense foreboding. If you have had this experience the problem is the drudgery goal was not magnetic—it was repulsive

Not all targets are the same. Some are easier to hit. Some are more fun, while others are dull and boring. Compelling targets have a magnetic force that pulls your efforts toward them, making them easier to hit. Many factors add to the magnetism of a goal to make it more compelling.

Wouldn't be great if you could set a goal and then it would pull you towards it like a powerful magnet would pull you? A pipe dream, you say? Well, magnetic goals do just that. Just imaging the goal-state—the time when you have achieved the goal—help you to move towards it.

A goal can be magnetic or repulsive. It is all in the crafting of the goal. Unfortunately, we're more likely to set repulsive goals than magnetic ones—especially when the goal involves stopping an activity or reducing something.

Make It Compelling

HOW YOUR SUBCONSCIOUS RESPONDS to a goal greatly influences its power. A compelling goal pulls you towards the goal; otherwise you must push yourself towards it. As soon as you push on yourself, resistance emerges. It's a natural response like putting out your hand when you are about to fall or like the way your dog pulls back when you pull on its collar.

Compelling goals are easier to achieve because they are positive. For one thing the brain processes positive information faster than negative information, which probably explains why double negatives are so confusing. Consider the following: "I've never resisted that" or "Don't not call if you won't be late." Such statements make us stop and shake our heads in confusion while we attempt to decipher their meaning.

Along the same lines, if you say to a young child, "Don't touch that vase", the child is likely to go straight for it. Why? Telling the child not to touch the vase creates an image of touching the vase in the child's mind! The same is true of your subconscious. For example, consider the imperative "Don't think of a pink elephant." What comes to mind? If you're like most people, an image of a pink elephant is in your mind while you attempt to not think of it. Like the child, the subconscious responds to images, and tends to delete negative modifiers.

Attractive vs. Repulsive Goals

THINKING OF YOUR GOAL brings its attractive or repulsive properties to mind. The trick in creating a magnetic goal—a goal that draws you toward it—is in specifying the goal in such a way that the images it brings to mind attract you. Attractive images attract. They are compelling and draw you to them.

A goal like "to lose 25 pounds" is likely to be resisted. Why? What do you have to do to lose weight? Eat less fries, less snacks, less steaks. Give up ice cream sundays. Eat salad without dressing. Exercise more, a lot more. To lose you must stop eating sweets and greasy foods (stopping pleasure) and push yourself to work out, which may be boring and painful. Such a goal is repulsive because you must force yourself to do what you are resisting.

Fortunately a repulsive goal can be transformed into a magnetic goal by creating an attractive image of the goal-state—the time when you achieve the goal.

The repulsive goal to lose 25 pounds can be transformed by sculpting an attractive image of what will happen when you have lost the 25 pounds—the goal-state. Simply ask: "What will you be doing when you have lost 25 pounds?" An answer might be, "looking good in a size 12 bathing suit". Seeing yourself looking good in a bathing suit is more compelling, than imagining not eating sweets and sweating at the gym. You are more likely to achieve a smaller waistline by imaging yourself in a size twelve swimsuit than thinking about foregoing delicious sweets.

Another common repulsive goal is "to manage time better by setting priorities," which conjures up a ho-hum image at best. Worse, you might see yourself with clipboards and checklists, which are probably repulsive images and sets avoidance motivation into motion.

A goal with a more compelling image might be "to spend at least one weekend a month in my lake side cabin," which is what you will be doing when you have become a better time manager. Imagining yourself relaxing at your cabin is more compelling than imaging making lists and checking them twice! Yet, to actually carve out the free time to go to your cabin might involve making lists, but doing so is not the picture of where you are going, it is just an intermediary step you must take to get there.

Negative Goals Repel

GOALS THAT CONTAIN NEGATIVE TARGETS are surprisingly common. Sometimes the goal was im-
posed on you by an authority like a parent or
teacher. Other times the goal appears positive until you check your Inner Compass to discover that
the doing level of the goal promotes burnout, not
bliss. Negative goals put you in a conflict situation, because success is defined in terms of activities or changes you dislike. Achieving such goals is
difficult. You will probably fail to achieve the goal
because the pictures in your mind repel you.

Some goals sound positive but contain hidden negative images. Sybil, an artist, said her goal
was "to increase billings by ten thousand dollars
a year". On the face of it, this seems like a positive goal. However, when asked how she felt when
biding her clients more money, she admitted that
she felt tremendously uncomfortable doing it.
This means that to reach her goal, Sybil must do
something she doesn't like doing several times a
year. If each biding were increased by $100, as-
suming every bid is accepted, she would have to
give 100 such bids in the following year to achieve
her goal. That's almost two times a week! The
mental picture of giving higher bids was repugnant
to Sybil and made her anxious just thinking about
it. To achieve her goal, Sybil would have to push
herself relentlessly. Goals with hidden negatives
like this thrust you into a cycle of self-prodding,
resistance and negativity. Worse, you learn that
you have a hard time doing what you want to do,
which diminishes your self-confidence.

Jeff, a plastic surgeon who runs a small clinic, had a similar dilemma. His goal was "to plan and implement eight marketing strategies in the coming year." Again the goal seemed positive, until Jeff described how he felt about selling. He cringed as he said he didn't like it at all! Marketing one's business is selling. So like Sybil, Jeff's seemingly positive goal was actually negative because it required him to sell himself which he doesn't like doing.

If Sybil and Jeff are to achieve their goals they must find compelling images and restate their goals to elicit the images when they think of their goals. As we all know, images are worth a thousand words. Much of our mental processing is in images. Empower your goal by creating an image of the moment when the goal is achieved—the goal-state.

See Yourself in the Goal-State

VAGUELY DEFINED GOALS such as "improving communications," "increasing satisfaction," or "having more fun", are difficult, perhaps impossible to achieve because they don't provide a clear picture of the target—the result you're shooting at. What does "improved communication" look like? How do you know when you've achieved it? Communications with whom? If you talk about politics with your husband after dinner, is that improved communications? Or does improved communications mean you respond to email faster? If so, how much faster? How long, how much and what quality of communication, with whom must be achieved before you can say your communications have improved?

Vaguely stated goals are frustrating because without a clear picture of the target you can miss hitting it. You may even be shooting at the wrong target altogether! How would you know if you don't know what the target looks like? Do this a few times and you can feel that you are constantly falling short in life. To be magnetic, the target must be clear enough that you can see yourself achieving the goal.

Use Your Imagination

SUPPOSE YOU SAY, "My goal is to be more assertive." What do you do? How do you start? To reach your goal, you must know what the hoped for result looks like. Imagining your goal creates a mental picture of it. The clearer the picture, and the more magnetic its draw, the better the goal can serve as a target so you can see what you are shooting for.

The more that you are able to see yourself achieving the goal, the greater its power. For example, "improved communications" can be translated into a specific picture, such as you discussing a "touchy" topic with your wife, reaching an understanding, followed by a romantic dinner. Put yourself into the scene, then notice how it feels. Then fix the picture of you being in "the goal state"—the time when you achieve the goal—and, again, study how

It is the imagination and not the will that is the dominating faculty of man. It is a serious mistake to advise people to train their wills; they should learn to control and direct their imaginations.

—Émille Coué

it feels. Then shape your picture of the goal-state
again. Continue this process until you create a
picture that is exactly what you are striving to
achieve. This is what makes the goal magnetic.

Engage Your Senses

MAKE YOUR GOAL VIBRANT and alive by engaging
all your senses. Research has demonstrated that
when more senses are engaged, more of the brain
is used. As it is used the brain's wiring actually
grows by developing thicker stems, or axioms, and
creating more complex connections, called syn-
apses, between the cells. What this means is that
what you think about and what you imagine estab-
lishes neural pathways, which are reinforced each
time you imagine that picture again.

Add Sensory Images

A GOAL-PICTURE such as seeing yourself playing
volleyball with friends on the beach can be made
more compelling by imaging the sounds of the
ocean waves, the seagulls cawing, your friends
laughing, and the slapping sound when hitting the
ball. Add in the sense of touch. Feel the warm
grainy sand under your feet and the weight of
the ball as you throw it up to serve it. Luxuriate
in the warm sun on your head and back. Notice
a refreshing breeze caressing your cheek. Smell
the salty air and the faint scent of perspiration.
Taste the refreshing flavor of the cold beer as you
gulp it down during the break. Add lots of visual
details. See a blue sky with wispy clouds forming
in the west. Notice what you and your friends are
wearing. See the volleyball coming towards you.

Notice the brand name written on the side of the ball as you hold it between plays.

Imagine your goal-picture often, each time add more sensory details to make the picture robust. Don't limit yourself to external details. Notice how you feel inside. What is your emotional state? Pay particular attention to joyful emotions, which add tremendously to the goal's magnetism. Just imaging your goal-picture for a few seconds sends impulses along neural pathways established when you first began creating your picture.

Be Specific

A SPECIFIC GOAL DESCRIBES what you will be doing when you achieve your goal—when you're in the "goal-state," which is the time in the future when you have achieved the goal. It is the solution to the problem you are solving, or a milestone you're striving to reach or an end-point in your project, or the achievement of something specific.

Go to the "doing level" of your goal. The doing level is seeing what you are actually doing when you've reached your goal. It includes actions, thoughts and feelings. Going to the doing level makes it easier to create a compelling picture.

Go to the Doing Level

CLOSE YOUR EYES and picture yourself in the goal-state—that time in the future when you have achieved your goal. Don't worry about how you'll achieve the goal; just imagine the time when the goal has been achieved. Don't force it. Just wait

and allow an image of you at the time you achieve
your goal to come to mind. When an image does
come to mind, don't judge it. Simply study it. Get
to know it.

What does being in the goal-state look like?
What are you doing? Who else is there? What are
they doing? What resources are used? What money? What people are involved? What technology?
Study the details of the image of you in the goal-
state. List on a paper or in your journal everything
you saw when imagining yourself in the goal-
state—especially those things you didn't expect.

Repeat the exercise several times until you
have created 5 or 6, or more, pictures of yourself having achieved your goal. For example, when
imagining the goal of "having fun," you might make
it more specific by seeing yourself in a comfortable chair enjoying the warmth of a fire in your
fireplace. In another scene you might see yourself
arranging beautiful flowers from your garden in
a vase. Another picture of having fun might be
seeing yourself chatting on the phone with a good
friend.

Take Small Steps

GOALS HAVE MARKERS or milestones, sometimes
called sub-goals or objectives, along the way to
the realization of the ultimate end and actual-
ization of what you are seeking. Breaking goals
into small steps makes them more manageable
and easier to achieve. The same principles apply
to these mini-goals. Just as your ultimate goals
should be powerful, so, too, your mini-goals will
be easier to achieve if they are powerful.

In addition to creating pictures of your end-goal, use compelling pictures to pull you towards your mini-goals. For example, if you were striving to get your masters degree (end-goal) you can create pictures of what you will be doing when you have a job requiring your degree and seeing your name on your business card with M.S. after it. You can also create pictures of the small steps you must take to get the masters degree, such as seeing yourself looking at the acceptance letter, or seeing yourself discussing your thesis with a professor.

Try It On

THIS SIMPLE ENVISIONING EXERCISE allows you to "try on" possible goals to see how they fit. Ask the question, "What will I be doing when I . . .?"

To be powerful, the goal must be a good fit like a comfortable shoe; otherwise you could be hobbled and unable to get anywhere. Notice sensations you experience when you imagine being in the goal-state. If it doesn't feel good, then change the picture until it does feel good. Experiment to discover what fits you. Work on the image of the goal-state until you find pictures where you feel energized and "one" with what you're doing. Use your Inner Compass. Keep refining your pictures until your Compass points towards bliss.

At first, it may be hard to keep your rational mind from doing its thing—judging. "That's no good!" "You should . . .!" or conjuring up "politically correct" pictures that may look good but don't necessarily fit you all that well. When this happens don't argue, just notice the thought and then set it aside.

A powerful goal is clear about what you will be doing when you achieve it. The more specifically you describe what you will be doing when you achieve the goal, the easier it is to create pictures of you doing it, the clearer your target will be. A clear target tells you where to aim and what to do and kicks in your intuition, which makes achieving your goal a lot easier.

Powerful Goals Say When

TIME LINES HELP you to bring the pieces together. Goals with no specific completion date make setting time lines for action steps difficult. Such open-ended goals undermine motivation and encourage procrastination. But a deadline must be realistic if the goal is to be powerful. Unrealistically short deadlines can trigger panic, provoking the opposite "Why bother?" attitude, and generally generate an oppressive climate. A deadline that is too short is usually better than no deadline at all. Unrealistic deadlines usually become apparent quickly, providing you an opportunity to readjust them to a more realistic time frame.

10

Work Smarter

THESE DAYS we have more work to do
than ever before. While computers promised
to lighten our work burden, because we can get
more done, we are expected to accomplish ever
more. There's no end in sight. We've all struggled
with the ever-increasing workload by working
harder and longer. It doesn't work. No matter how
much you accomplish there's more to do. That
strategy may have worked for a while, but the
flow of work is endless. There just aren't enough
hours in the day to do everything. The more you
do, the more there is to do. To succeed these
days you must work smarter, not harder.

Sure, you've heard that platitude before. But
how? Where to start? leveraging holds the key to
working smarter.

Use Leverage

A LEVER ENABLES YOU TO EXERT a lesser effort to
lift a larger load than you could lift by simply picking the
item up. Applying leveraging to your workload means that
you put your efforts into those activities and projects that
get the greatest results and delegate, out-source or leave
undone those things that bring less results.

To apply leveraging to your work, you must know what you are to achieve and the impact that each of your activities has upon that achievement.

When you have identified the purpose that you are to achieve, the next challenge is to determine how much impact your various activities have on accomplishing your purpose. Apply the 80-20 Rule to decide which activities to focus on and which to delegate.

Give me a place to stand and a lever long enough and I will move the world.

—Archimedes

The 80/20 Rule

THE 80-20 RULE STATES that eighty percent of your output comes from twenty percent of your input. The Vital Few and Trivial Many Rule, as it is sometimes called, can be applied to almost anything. For example, Richard Koch reported in his book, *The 80/20 Principle*, that twenty percent of motorists cause eighty percent of auto accidents and that twenty percent of criminals account for eighty percent of the value of all crime. On a personal level, Koch says we wear twenty percent of our clothes eighty percent of the time. Employing the 80-20 Rule can help you to manage yourself excellently.

Sales managers know that eighty percent of sales come from twenty percent of sales calls. Importantly, the converse is that eighty percent of sales calls yields only twenty percent of the sales. A sales person, for example, does not get the same result from each call. Most calls—the trivial many—bring in little or no sales, whereas a few calls—the vital few—hit it big. Whether or not the break down is exactly 80/20 doesn't matter. What matters is that much of what we do yields only ho hum results. The trick to working smarter when it comes to sales is to identify the accounts that yield the big sales and then to concentrate on selling to them.

For entrepreneurs, finding the 80/20 ratios is crucial for maximizing performance. Identify the products or services that generate the most income—the 20%. Market these and drop those that sell slowly—the 80%. Work on the parts of your business that you can improve significantly with your core skills and outsource projects outside your prime skills to other people. Work hardest on elements that work hardest for you. Reward well your best employees, transition out the worst. Phase out bad clients and focus on improving service and/or selling to the best clients.

The value of 80-20 Rule for self-managers is that it reminds you to focus on the twenty percent that matters. Of the things you do during your day, only twenty percent produce most of

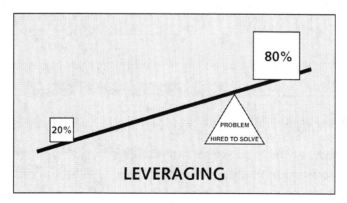

your results. The depressing corollary is that 80% of your efforts yield only 20% of your results. Talk about a rat wheel!

It is not necessary to do extraordinary things to get extraordinary results.

—Warren Buffett

This high-effort/low-results work generally revolves around routine, busy work and meetings.

If you can identify the twenty percent activities that yield eighty percent of your results, you can apply leverage to those high yield activities and get a bigger result. In leveraging, we endeavor to use a lesser effort to life a larger load than we could lift by simply picking the item up. The secret of leveraging lives in the 80-20 Rule.

Identifying key factors for success can be difficult. Begin by dissecting your job into projects, activities, major steps and desired results as imaginatively as possible down into smaller pieces or segments. Next rate each segment on how much impact it has on solving the problem that you were hired to solve, or upon achieving your purpose in pursuing a project. The higher the impact, the greater the mileage, the more results. Knowing what you are expected to accomplish helps tremendously in identifying your key factors for success. The key factors for success are the twenty percent activities that will yield the greatest results. These are the priority activities.

Problem You Were Hired to Solve

KNOWING YOUR PURPOSE facilitates working smarter because you use it to measure the 80-20 Rule against. The first step is to identify the problem you were hired to solve as discussed in Chapter 8. When you have a very clear picture of the actual problem that is your responsibility, then do an inventory of your activities. Over several days, list everything that you do vis-a-vis work. Take some time with this so that you can see what you actually spend time doing.

Next, apply the 80-20 Rule to each activity. You can do this by weighing how much impact each activity has upon solving the problem you were hired to solve on a scale from 1 to 9, with 1 being little impact and 9, being great impact. Then circle all the activities that you rated as 6 to 9 as 80% activities. These are high priority activities and get you the most mileage. Completing these activities is working smarter.

Activities you rated as 1 to 3 are 20% activities that have little impact upon solving your assigned problem. Delegate these activities or don't do them at all. Take another look at activities that you rated 4-6. Some you may move into the 80% group; others into the 20% group.

Other Work Smarter Tips

WHEN POSSIBLE, reuse past work so that you get double the mileage for the same effort. A related strategy is one task, many goals. Look for other goals that can also be satisfied with the same task? For example, you may be writing a report. Perhaps you can pull out a few paragraphs to post on your blog.

Keep in mind that most things don't need to be "good", just "good enough" to meet the objective.

Little is gained by refining. Instead move on to another task.

Concentrate on quality of work over quantity. The person who builds a career on doing the most work commits to living on a treadmill. The work will never be done, and you will become known among your co-workers as someone who never turns down an assignment. Read: dumping ground. Quality is what matters. People don't lose a job for not working unpaid overtime, they lose a job for not performing well at the most important times; and a resume is a list of big accomplishments, not of hours worked.

Focus on your strengths. You will be most productive when your work draws on your strengths. Identify your strengths so that you don't waste time working on things, which give you only small return. To be effective, you should do only a few things, the things you are very good at. Only do things you are best at doing; delegate or outsource the rest.

Use your work rhythms. Some people work best alone, others are most productive with people and background noise. Some people are most productive in the morning while some others are most productive in the evening. Identify your work rhythms and then arrange your work accordingly. Pay attention to your internal clock and figure out when your energy is highest. Do routine things during your down time.

Take high-profile projects. If you just take the grunt work, your boss might or might not appreciate it, but it certainly won't make you a star and you won't go very far. Instead, volunteer for the big projects, the ones that will make a name for both you and your company. If there aren't any available, make your own. Be sure you can do them well, and these projects can have a huge impact on your life. If you take on high-impact projects, you can be more productive working a half-day than if you worked ten hours on a task that has little impact.

11

Pursue Excellence

A RISTOTLE BELIEVED that no one set of absolute standards can determine the excellent action in every situation because each situation is unique. Excellence, in Aristotle's view, is carrying out the right action at the right time.

You Become What You Do

ARISTOTLE BELIEVED it is inappropriate to answer the question "What kind of person is he or she?" by saying, "He is talented" or "She is intelligent." To Aristotle, such qualities are incidental to the question; instead he believed that we reveal who we are by what we do.

"The creation and the destruction of any virtue are effected by identical causes and identical means.... It is as a result of playing the harp that harpers become good or bad in their art. The same is true of builders and all other craftsmen. Men will become good builders as a result of building well, and bad builders as a result of building badly.... Now this holds also of the virtues. It is in the course of our dealings with our fellow-men that we become just or unjust. It is our behavior in a crisis and our habitual reactions

We are what we repeatedly do. Excellence, then, is not an act, but a habit."

—Aristotle

*Excellence is doing ordinary   to danger that make
things extraordinarily well.   us brave or cow-
—John W. Gardner   ardly, as it may be.
So with our desires
and passions. Some men are made temperate and
gentle, other profligate and passionate, the former
by conducting themselves in one way, the latter by
conducting themselves in another, in situations in
which their feelings are involved."*

The Right Action

ARISTOTLE BELIEVED THAT ALL THINGS in nature have
an innate tendency in the direction of the best
condition of which they are capable. An acorn, for
example, grows into the best oak tree possible
given its genetic makeup, conditions of the soil
and climate.

The best possible condition of humans is happiness. But happiness is not the accumulation of
material goods, having fun, or winning acclaim.
While each of us has the potential for happiness,
but attaining it does not come automatically.
Happiness, as we all know, cannot be purchased
or given. Aristotle says, "Fortune can supply the
happy man with the means, and create for him
the conditions of his happiness; it cannot create
his happiness." Achieving happiness depends upon
ourselves—how we act, the way that we handle
the everyday challenges of living.

Aristotle believed that happiness comes from
becoming the best possible self that we can be.
To do this, we must strive for and achieve what
Aristotle calls "goodness," which is excellence.
Excellence is not a grade or a ranking; it is the

way in which we handle daily situations—the tests of life. We pass the tests when we carry out the right action—the excellent response. For each situation, which is unique, there is a right action, at the right time and to the right degree. Carrying out this "right action" is excellence.

Knowing The Right Action

HOW DO WE DETERMINE THE EXCELLENT ACTION? Aristotle offers a flexible standard for determining excellence—the golden mean, which is the right action, at the right time, in the right measure. He says:

"It is in the nature of moral qualities that they can be destroyed by deficiency on the one hand and excess on the other. We can see this in the instances of bodily health and strength. Physical strength is destroyed by too much and also by too little exercise. Similarly health is ruined by eating or drinking either too much or too little, while it is produced, increased, and preserved by taking the right quantity of drink and victuals.

"Well, it is the same with temperance, courage, and the other virtues. The

> There is nothing so useless as doing efficiently that which should not be done at all.
>
> — Peter F. Drucker

man who shuns and fears everything and can stand up to nothing becomes a coward. The man who is afraid of nothing at all, but marches up to every danger, becomes foolhardy. In the same way the man who indulges in every pleasure without refraining from a single one becomes incontinent. If, on the other hand, a man behaves like the Boor in comedy and turns his back on every pleasure, he will find his sensibilities becoming blunted. So also temperance and courage are destroyed both by excess and by deficiency, and they are kept alive by observation of the mean.

"By "goodness" [or excellence] I mean goodness of moral character, since it is moral goodness that deals with feelings and actions, and it is in them that we find excess, deficiency, and the mean. It is possible, for example, to experience fear, boldness, desire, anger, pity, and pleasures and pain generally, too much or too little or to the right amount. If we feel them too much or too little, we are wrong. But to have these feelings at the right times on the right occasions towards the right people for the right motive and in the right way is to have them in the right measure, that is, somewhere between the extremes; and this is what characterizes goodness."

Excellence is the Right Action

IN ANY SITUATION, there is a continuum of possible actions between two extremes. Excellence is that action, somewhere in the middle, that is the right way to feel, the right way to act, with this person, at this time, under these circumstances.

As Archimedes said, "Give me a fulcrum upon which to place a lever and I shall move the world." The golden mean is the fulcrum in human action and, when found, yields great power—excellence. For warriors, excellence is the right blow at just the right time.

Live Impeccably

ARISTOTLE WAS NOT ALONE in emphasizing the importance of striving for excellence. When Don Juan taught Carlos the Way of the Warrior, he stressed excellence—living impeccably, as he called it.

SHOELACES

Don Juan and Carlos were walking through a steep ravine when Don Juan stopped to tie his shoelaces. Just then a huge boulder came thundering down and landed several feet in front of them—right where they would have been, had they not stopped.

"Don Juan, if you hadn't stopped to tie your laces, we would have been crushed!" Carlos mused.

Don Juan used the event to teach Carlos a lesson in living impeccably. "Suppose we stopped to tie my shoelaces and by doing so we had gained a precious moment that saved us from being crushed by that boulder."

Don Juan hesitated, then continued, "Suppose, on another day in another ravine, we stopped to tie my shoelaces and by doing so we lost a precious moment and were crushed by the boulder. What should we do?"

Flustered, Carlos stammered, "Well, I don't know. You never know when a boulder might crush you!"

"Exactly!" Don Juan exclaimed. "That's why
the only possible freedom in the ravine con-
sists in my tying my shoelaces impeccably."

—Carlos Castaneda
The Second Ring of Power

Means and Extremes

EXCELLENCE IS THE "RIGHT ACTION" at the right
time, to the right degree. The right action is not
fixed, it changes. Excellence is that just right action between extremes possibilities—the mean,
which moves along a continuum between the extremes, varying from situation to situation. Finding that mean and carrying out the right action
at the right time is the art of managing yourself
for excellence. Each dilemma is an opportunity to
practice excellence.

Extreme	Mean
Impetuosity — Ambivalence	Decisiveness
Passivity — Aggressiveness	Assertiveness
Fearfulness — Rashness	Adventurousness
Miserliness — Extravagance	Money Management
Self-Depreciation — Bragging	Self-Presentation
Self-Denial — Indulgence	Self-Management
Conformity — Rebellion	Autonomy
Obsequiousness — Surliness	Conviviality

Let's consider a couple of extremes. Wrestling
with assertiveness is a problem for many, especially women. Typically socialized to be passive,
with few assertive models to emulate, women

often go to the other extreme, becoming aggressive in misguided attempts to be assertive. Some women struggling with this dichotomy rigidly adhere to a hard line, pouncing on any and all remarks or actions that might be construed as put-downs. Although there are many times

If you don't do it with excellence, don't do it at all! Because if it's not excellent, it won't be profitable or fun, and if you're not in business for fun or profit, what the hell are you doing there?

— Robert Townsend

when a woman should confront demeaning behavior, an all-or-nothing rule is rarely an effective guide. Too often it is overkill, in which she wins the battle and loses the war. Instead, each situation should be responded to on its particulars. There are times when another's action is a put-down, but it's to her long-run benefit to let it pass without response; other times she may be being hypersensitive, seeing what is not there; while sometimes it is imperative that she speak out.

But judging when to act is only part of the challenge. She must also determine how to act. Should she confront the offender? Leave the situation? Report the affront? Or quietly change the parameters of the situation? An excellent action requires many considerations.

Men, on the other hand, have their struggles with the extremes of reason and emotion. Socialized to think and not feel, many men have difficulty finding a mean in which they are both sensitive and masculine.

We must not, in trying to think about how we can make a big difference, ignore the small daily differences we can make which, over time, add up to big differences that we often cannot foresee.

—Marian Wright Edelman

Another example is self-managing, which is an ongoing challenge for all of us. While some of us have had the fortune of having acquired good self-management skills from parents, few of us have ever had any direct training. In fact, many take self-management—also called self-control or self-discipline—to mean withholding pleasure and applying other forms of punishment to oneself. But self-denial is just as much an extreme as overindulgence.

Being able to motivate ourselves to do things that we don't care to do; knowing when and where and to what degree to pleasure ourselves; knowing when to work and when to play are all components of self-management.

Good self-managers can work in unstructured and unrewarding situations by creating their own goals and rewards. They can self-start and keep themselves going. Poor self-managers, on the other hand, depend on others to start them, to set their goals, and to dole out their rewards. In short, poor self-managers depend upon others for motivation.

Judicious money management is another challenge. Executives who pinch every penny by meeting clients in the office rather than spending allotted expense accounts or by saving paper clips and scraps of paper are as bad as those who constantly go over budget or authorize needless expenditures.

Each day presents opportunities to tackle the challenge of finding the golden mean and determining the excellent action. We can never completely master the challenge of excellence but can strive to become increasingly proficient.

THERE IS A SEASON

For everything there is a season,
And a time for every matter under heaven:
A time to be born, and a time to die;
A time to plant, and a time to pluck up what is
planted;

A time to kill, and a time to heal;
A time to break down, and a time to build up;
A time to weep, and a time to laugh;
A time to mourn, and a time to dance;
A time to throw away stones, and a time to
gather stones together;
A time to embrace, And a time to refrain from
embracing;

A time to seek, and a time to lose;
A time to keep, and a time to throw away;
A time to tear, and a time to sew;
A time to keep silence, and a time to speak;
A time to love, and a time to hate,
A time for war, and a time for peace.

—Ecclesiastes 3:1-8

12

Use Wisdom

THE FACULTY REQUIRED to determine the golden mean—the excellent action—is wisdom. Aristotle, in his discourses, identified two types of wisdom—theoretical and practical. We must develop and utilize each to actualize our potential.

Theoretical Wisdom

THEORETICAL WISDOM is formal knowledge we acquire from education—what we learn in school, from the media, from books, and from experts. These are the facts we know to be true, or at least believe to be true. Knowing that a balanced diet is essential for health is theoretical wisdom, for example. Similarly, knowing we must be decisive rather than ambivalent or impetuous when faced with a decision is theoretical wisdom. Theoretical wisdom is what we ordinarily think of as intellectual knowledge. But it is not limited solely to facts we are told or have read in a book.

Theoretical wisdom is general information and universal truths we draw upon when we contemplate ends or goals and our strategies for achieving them. Theoretical wisdom tells us that happiness is an actualized life, for example, and that we actualize our potential through excellent actions.

Intuition

THEORETICAL WISDOM comes also from intuitive reasoning, which is part of our intelligence that enables us to grasp fundamental principles. For example, we are engaging in intuitive reasoning when, after experiencing a given number of instances, we suddenly catch on to the generalization present in those examples.

Intuitive reasoning is that part of our intelligence that enables us to figure things out for ourselves—the "aha" of insight into the fundamentals of the situation. For example, by observing the behavior of falling objects, Newton grasped the law of gravity. Or if from watching others interact we gain the insight that others tend to like us when we show interest in them, we are using intuitive reasoning powers. This insight about people then is added to our theoretical wisdom—things we know.

Successful business strategies result not from rigorous analysis but from a particular state of mind, in what I call the mind of the strategist, insight and a consequent drive for achievement, often amounting to a sense of mission, fuels thought process which is basically creative and intuitive rather than rational. Strategists do not reject analysis. Indeed they hardly can do without it. But they use it only to stimulate the creative process, to test the ideas that emerge, to work out their strategic implications, or to ensure successful execution of high potential "wild" ideas that might otherwise never be imple-

mented properly. Great strategies, like great works of art or great scientific discoveries, call for technical mastery in the working out but originate in insights that are beyond the reach of conscious analysis.

—Kenichi Ohmae
The Mind of the Strategist

Use Intuition

INTUITION IS A SECRET SKILL of the successful. Intuition is a direct, and seemingly spontaneous, "knowing" about something but not knowing how you know. It is an "ah ha!" or an immediate comprehension about a situation that provides a gestalt or understanding about the whole of the situation as compared to examining its parts, creating a kind of holographic knowing. It is an insight about the whole of the situation.

Intuitive knowing comes as a spark or a trace of an idea. Information bubbles up. Intuition speaks to us through symbols and images rather than in words and concepts. Messages are fleeting and subtle, more easily heard when the mind and body are calm. Intuitive knowing can contradict physical facts and what everyone else believes to be true. It is a sensing. Listening to intuition is an act of faith—faith in your own wisdom. "I know what I know!" Phrases like "My gut tells me," "It feel right," and "A light bulb went off" all indicate an intuitive process in action.

Our minds are busy thinking all the time. Intuition is a kind of behind the scenes thinking that is going on when you are paying attention to something else. Intuition rarely lies. The challenge is to tune into intuitive knowing, to decipher its meaning and to have the faith in what we "know" to act upon it.

Become Receptive

WHEN REVVED UP with our minds going a mile a minute, we don't hear intuitive messages. To tune into intuition we need to calm down and listen. Pick a time and place with the minimum of distractions and make yourself comfortable. Using any method you prefer, slow yourself down.

Smooth, slow, deep breathing facilitates receiving intuitive guidance. Make your in breaths the same length as the out breaths and thinking of your breathing in and out as one continuous smooth loop helps. Quietly notice thoughts, ideas and hunches that come. Notice feelings and images. Notice what you know. Don't strain. Don't judge. Just notice.

Ask a Question

TAP INTO INTUITION BY ASKING A QUESTION. When you sit silently and focus on a particular concern stated as a question, images come to mind, seemingly of their own accord. You can ask a question aloud, silently in your mind, write it on a paper or type it into your computer. Then sit quietly; still your mind. Wait patiently and notice hunches, thoughts and ideas, and especially images that come into your mind. Intuition communicates in images and associations.

Use Associations

WRITE DOWN WHAT CAME TO MIND. Don't worry about it making sense or about it being related to your question. Just jot down thoughts and words that came to mind. Especially important: note images that came to you. Also, note physical sensations and emotions you may have experienced.

Hidden in your notes may be an "answer" to your question. The challenge is to understand its meaning. The intuitive mind works by associations—this reminds-you-of-that-type of thinking. Read over your notes. For each important word or phrase that you noted, notice what associations come into your mind while thinking about it. Write these down. Do the same thing for the images. Repeat the process with the new words and images. For example, an image of a rainbow might bring to mind pot of gold, sun after the storm, and Wizard of Oz. Then each of these images can trigger further associations. It is a kind of thinking that is not logic based—but powerful thinking nonetheless, one that dips into your wisdom.

One approach is to make up a "reading" about your question from your hunches, images and associations similar to the way in which a fortune teller does in reading Tarot cards, for example. Skeptical? Try it. Use the images and associations to tell a story about the question. You'll be amazed at the wisdom regarding your question that comes through. It is a powerful device.

Incubate

GATHER HARD INFORMATION about your concern, then ask your question and incubate. Let it cook.

Do something else. Don't think about it for a while—even a few days. Just pay attention to what you notice. There are infinite things in the world to catch your attention. What you notice is not coincidence—meaning is attached to it. Every sign, every act, every deed, everything we notice has some significance.

People who try incubation report amazing experiences in coming across the "answer." Having a book fall off the shelf in a bookstore or library, picking it up to find the book open to a page that addresses the issue is a surprisingly common experience. Other incubation experiences include flashes of inspiration that come while showering or a message in a dream. You must be receptive to catch these answers, however.

Know What You Know

OTHER-DIRECTED PEOPLE are highly influenced by what other people think and do. They tend to set aside what they know in favor of what the peer group thinks—the politically correct opinion. Autonomy, on the other hand, requires a distance from the peer group, an ability to know what you know and to have faith in your own knowing—especially when it deviates from popular opinion or is politically incorrect.

Practical Wisdom

THEORETICAL WISDOM DOESN'T HELP with the particulars, however. How do we show interest in this particular person so that he or she will like us? What is too obsequious? Too surly? Where is the golden mean? For these answers, we need practical wisdom

Practical wisdom is sound judgment in practical situations. It is prudence, the capacity or habit of deliberating well about what is good and advantageous to oneself. It's exercising high levels of emotional intelligence (EQ). Practical wisdom involves carefully attending to all circumstances that may relate to an action. It is being aware—being mindful.

Good Deliberation

GOOD DELIBERATION, however, does not depend on a long process of reasoning. It is the product of applying theoretical wisdom including intuition to particular circumstances. It is the habit of correctly sizing things up, of evaluating the problem at hand in terms of its general characteristics, and then deciding the way this particular situation is to be handled and the time it is to be done. Practical wisdom is the direct appraisal of the situation and of the excellent action.

In sum, whereas theoretical wisdom is developed through education, practical wisdom comes from experience. Theoretical wisdom helps us understand universal principles and situations in the abstract; practical wisdom helps us determine how to act in particular situations.

Be Mindful

THE PRIMARY OBSTACLE to practical wisdom is what the Eastern philosophers call "being asleep" or going through our daily lives reacting to situations with our minds elsewhere—living mindlessly. Practical wisdom requires that we be conscious and pay attention—that we are mindful.

To the samurai, being fully alert—mindful—while assessing the circumstances meant the difference between a long or short life. At any moment, there could be a razor sharp sword chop from an unexpected opponent. The martial arts master trained the student to pay attention to everything in the moment by unexpectedly jumping out and applying a painful whack to any exposed area and admonishing the student to "be here now!"

THE WHACK

He was carrying the last of two brimming buckets up the mountain path. The blow came from behind and landed squarely across his right ear. The tremendous pain was like looking into the sun. He blinked and found himself on the ground. The buckets where rolling happily back down the mountain and the Old Man was looking down at him with great satisfaction....

There were three more attacks before supper. By then the boy was so jumpy that he decided against eating. Ordered to come in, however, he obeyed....

They ate in their usual silence then the Old Man said to him through the twilight, "An animal will jump at every sound, a leaf in the wind, a falling cone. A disciplined man will move only when it is necessary." There was a ruminative pause, then the addendum: "The moment before it is necessary...."

Thereafter, he never turned his back on the Old Man again. He might be carrying a load of wood, reading a sutra or helpless in the bathing barrel, but part of his mind was always alert for the vicious stick of bamboo....

Yet in time he found it possible to duck instead of dive, to veer and not drop the wood, the water, or the book. He was almost surprised to find it was possible to move with caution and still get all of his chores done in good time.

Then no longer did he merely pass through a door thinking of something else. It became an act of dangerous importance. Nor did he round a corner unthinkingly, approach the top of a hill blithely, nor pass closely by a tree. Reverie was replaced by exquisite attention to what he was doing. Each act called for total concentration if he was to avoid pain, a fall of pride and the tattoo of a bruise. So, to avoid the hurt, he learned to perceive everything that is Now.

—William Dale Jennings
The Ronin

Be alert, use your practical wisdom here in this situation, now, rather than letting your mind wander elsewhere or reacting emotionally without deliberation.

13

Think Like a Warrior

MOST OF US WOULD PROBABLY PREFER to have a preponderance of positive emotions and pleasant sensations in our lives. Yet, all too often we succumb to a kind of thinking that creates anger, depression, and anxiety and, try as we may to think positively, negative, stress-producing thinking triumphs.

It is easy to believe that the cause of downer emotions is external, out there somewhere, caused by something somebody else did, or didn't do. However, emotions are usually triggered by what we think about situation, the actual words and not the situation at all. How often do you hear yourself thinking, "He made me mad," for example? Another person cannot *make* you mad. Events cannot make you respond.

What actually happens is that when an event occurs we evaluate it as positive or negative, good or bad, safe or threatening. Although we are constantly making such appraisals, we were largely unaware of them. Following is a classic example.

Sitting in front of a lovely fire, reading an enjoyable novel, you feel relaxed, comfortable and secure. Out of the corner of your eye, without being consciously aware that you are looking, you notice something move. Suddenly you leap several

> *A disciplined mind leads to happiness. An undisciplined mind leads to suffering.*
>
> —The Dalai Lama

feet from the chair filled with fear with your heart pounding. As you land, you realize that it is was nothing more than a draft moving the window curtain, and you think, "Oh, it was nothing." Seeing there is no danger, you calm down and return to the novel.

Undoubtedly, you have experienced a variation of this scenario. It demonstrates two things. First, our minds are constantly alert, checking out the environment, alert for possible threats.

Second, we make rapid evaluations of events, the most basic being: "Is there a threat?" Anytime our minds determine that, yes, indeed there is a threat, then the stress response instantly kicks in, mobilizing us to fight or flee. All of this occurs without any conscious thought.

We are appraising things all the time, and yet, as the story illustrates, we are largely unaware of it. We evaluate others' motives, too. For example, the head of a pharmaceuticals lab in one of my workshops described how his technicians often "capriciously" argued with his introducing new tests. He said it

> Don Juan: *The most effective way to live is as a warrior. Worry and think before you make any decision, but once you make it, be on your way free from worries and thoughts; there will be a million other decisions still awaiting you. That's the warrior's way.*
>
> —Carlos Castaneda
> *A Separate Reality*

made him feel angry. I pointed out that "capri-
cious" was his interpretation of their actions and
not necessarily reflective of the tech's motives.
Perhaps their arguing resulted from the natural
tendency of people to question and resist change.

Later this man reported that when he thought,
"I should expect resistance to change," instead of,
"They're playing with me and deliberately trying
to sabotage my program," he no longer responded
with anger. Instead, he saw that helping them to
accept new tests was a challenging part of his
responsibility.

Constant Self-Improvement

WARRIORS SEEK CONSTANT SELF-IMPROVEMENT. Warriors are ordinary people who though hard training
become capable of extraordinary feats of courage—something that was impossible unless they
were able to overcome the fears, hesitations,
doubts, and second thoughts that plague anyone
going into battle.

The Japanese warriors—the samurai—looked at
challenges in terms of outer opponents and inner opponents. All inner opponents are dragons—
obstacles that prevent us from doing our best to
win our battles. Assume the frontal position and
confronting inner dragons head-on.

Don Juan: *An impeccable stalker can turn anything into pray .... We can even stalk our own weaknesses ....*  *You figure out your routines until you know all of the doing of your weaknesses and then you come upon them and pick them up like rabbits inside a cage.*

—Carlos Castaneda
The Second Ring of Power

Practice Under-Reacting

NEGATIVE SELF-TALK BLOWS THINGS UP and out of proportion to the actual danger at hand. This type of self-talk is not helpful. Self-talk that generates anxiety gets in the way of solving problems and encourages avoidance. Helpful self-talk, the way a coach would talk to you is more balanced and often down plays the risks in the situation. Lucinda Basset refers to this down playing self-talk as "under-reactive statements" as compared to the negative self-talk that triggers over-reacting. Following are several example of under-reactive statements.

Under-Reactive Statements

This is no big deal.

No sweat!

This will pass.

It just doesn't matter.

I'm taking this too seriously.

It's just anxiety. It will go away.

It's not my problem.

This is not worth getting anxious over.

It's only money.

This isn't an emergency.

Don't sweat the small stuff.

This isn't the worst thing that can happen.

Tomorrow will be a better day.

Ten years from now I won't remember this.

This is excitement, not anxiety.

Just do it.

So what?

When you let negative self-talk like "Oh, no! What will I do?" or "Oh, my gawd, this is awful!" take over, your emotional brain believes you are facing a real crisis and goes on alert. But most situations are not a disaster requiring that you mobilize yourself for a crisis. Furthermore, it's easier to function in difficult situations, even emergencies, when you are calmer than when you are panicking. When you talk to yourself with under-reactive statements you react less. Your thinking is clearer so that you can focus on the problem at hand and think it through more easily. While negative self-talk tends to use over-reactive statements, coaching talk uses under-reactive statements like those in the list.

When you catch yourself getting worked up, stop and ask yourself, "How can I under-react? How can I take this situation less seriously? Remember, to ask the question in the way that a supportive friend would ask it.

Use Coping Statement

COACHING TALK SUBSTITUTES "coping statements" for the fuss-budget's alarming self-talk. Coping statements emphasize what you can do, rather than what you can't do. Like the under-reactive statements, coping statements help you to stay calm and feel in control rather than helpless. The distinction between the two types of statements is not real clear and not terribly important. What is important is catching the negative self-talk early on and substituting coaching talk with under-reactive or coping statements.

Coping Statements

I can handle this.

This is an opportunity.

I can ride this out.

I can take all the time I need.

There's no need to push myself.

I feel nervous which is natural
in a situation like this.

I've survived worse than this before.

I'm relaxed and feeling calm.

I can't please everyone.

I'm proud of myself.

I'm not in a hurry.

I have plenty of time.

Anxiety won't hurt me

Resisting won't help.

No pain, no gain.

Feeling helpless and victimized by the situation generates anxiety and fear. Coaching talk with coping statements, on the other hand, cultivates an attitude of mastery and self-control, a feeling of I-Can-Do which builds confidence and self-esteem.

There are a number of ways to incorporate coping and under-reactive statements into your self-coaching talk. But before you can do that you have to get used to hearing yourself using coaching talk. Some people like to pick out one statement that has particular meaning to them and saying it over and over, almost like a mantra. "I can handle this." "I can handle this." "I can handle this." Or "There's no need to push myself." "There's no need to push myself." "There's no need to push myself." This is particularly effective when combined with slow, deep breathing. Try this and you'll discover that you will soon feel calmer and more empowered—more in control.

Saying a coping statement over and over to yourself while breathing deeply and slowly helps to program your emotional brain.

Another technique which I highly recommend is to place a check mark next to the coping and under-reactive statements that could fit your situation. Rewrite these statements in a list in your journal. What statements can you add to the list? Write these down on the list in your journal. Get a package of file cards and rewrite the statements from your list, one per file card. Read the statements on the cards several times a day. You can carry the cards with you in your purse or suit pocket. Anytime you're stuck waiting, for example, pull out your cards and read a few coping statements. Do this for several days. Add cards whenever you think of a new statement.

Substitute Coaching Talk

AFTER YOU HAVE FAMILIARIZED YOURSELF with coping and under-reactive statements for several days so that they are on the tip of your tongue, then you can begin simple substitution. First you must catch yourself in negative self-talk.

When you hear the negative self-talk say, "STOP!" very loudly inside your head. Some people find it helps to imagine a stop sign stopping the worrisome thoughts

Ask yourself, "What can I say that is more soothing? What would I say to comfort someone else? What would a personal trainer say to me now?" If you have been reading over the coping statements, one or more should easily come to mind. Formulate a soothing, comforting comment to say to yourself. Deliberately say these things to yourself. Self-coaching will feel artificial and forced at first, but do it anyway.

You can cultivate positive emotions by changing the stories you tell yourself about the events in your life. Do you cast yourself in the role of victim, blaming others or external circumstances for your problems. Most people do. Becoming aware of the difference between the facts in a given situation and the way you interpret those facts can be powerful in itself. You have a choice about how to view a given event. The story you tell yourself about the event powerfully influences the emotions you feel. Make it a practice to tell the most hopeful and personally empowering story possible in any given situation, without denying or minimizing the facts.

There are three lenses for viewing the story in different perspective from that of the victim. With the reverse lens, ask yourself, "What would the other person in this interaction say and in what ways might that be true?" With the long lens ask, "How will I most likely view this situation in six months?" With the wide lens ask yourself, "Regardless of the outcome of this issue, how can I grow and learn from it?"

Practicing viewing situations from these three perspectives takes discipline. You can intentionally cultivate positive emotions.

14

Manage Stress

THE WORD STRESS, as we know it, was first used by Hans Selye to refer to a cluster of physiological responses—including increased heart rate and adrenaline level, muscle tension, quickening of breath—he called the "general adaptation syndrome." He called it a general syndrome because the same pattern of changes occurs in response to a wide variety of events.

> *When Heaven is about to confer a great office upon a man, it first exercises his mind with suffering, and his sinews and bones with toil; it exposes him to poverty and confounds all his undertakings. Then it is seen if he is ready.*
>
> —Moshe

Triggered by Threats

STRESSFUL EVENTS have one thing in common—an element of threat. The physiological changes occurring during the stress response are in preparation either to fight the threat or flee from it.

The stress response is "adaptive" because it helps us to adapt, to survive. When we overcome or avoid the threat, we survive; if we fail to fight or to flee, dire consequences usually ensue.

It is not possible to eliminate all stress, nor is it desirable to attempt to do so. Selye emphasized that stress is a beneficial and essential life process, intimately involved in physical development and in learning.

State of Readiness

THE STRESS RESPONSE is an all-stops-pulled state of readiness, preparing us to move quickly and forcefully. Problems occur, however, when we remain in this state of physiological arousal for too long—when we do not defeat or in get away from the threat or when there are an overwhelming number of threats—changes—to confront. Our bodies are not constructed to tolerate a state of readiness for long periods of time. Resources and defenses wear down, leading to detrimental health problems and psychological dysfunction.

The relationship between stress and performance is curvilinear, not linear. What the chart illustrates is that when stress levels or tension is low, performance tends to be low as well. There is too little stimulation to be able to keep atten-

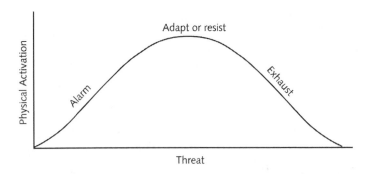

The General Adaptation Syndrome

tion on what is at hand. This is commonly considered to be boredom, under stimulation, or depression.

At high levels of stress, performance is also low, because stress impairs physical and intellectual functioning. This state is often experienced as spinning our wheels. High stress interferes with creative performance and is signaled by hyperactivity, forgetfulness, frequent mistakes, lack of concentration, and irritability.

Because of the complexity of the modern world and the difficulties we encounter at work, as well as the increasing pace of change in our lives, most of us experience chronic high stress.

Maintain Balance

THE OBJECTIVE OF STRESS MANAGEMENT is to keep stress or tension levels within the optimal range for performance, health, and well being. That is, when bored or depressed, we should increase tension levels by listening to upbeat music, for example, or taking a cold shower, jogging, working in peopled areas such as the cafeteria, or even eating hot spicy foods all of which are stimulating activities.

For most of us, however, the problem is being too tense and we can expect it to continue, as we must cope with increasing change. So it behooves you to know a number of ways to bring the stress level down into the optimal range.

It's a mistake to attempt to reduce stress by trying to avoid change. Although a natural tendency, avoidance is not acting in your best interest. If we are to grow and move forward as we navigate the limbo state between the old and the new, we must be able to tolerate a certain degree of stress. To move forward step by step, we must pick up the foot behind to swing it to the stepping stone ahead. Movement always supposes a letting go of the past position.

Stress Buffers

STRESS BUFFERS shield us from its toxic effects. Feeling that you are in control, relaxation, a strong social support group, and having fun.

Relax

RELAXATION IS A POWERFUL STRESS ANTIDOTE. It is a regenerative process—a time of rest and refueling. Although it seems like the natural thing to do when tense, surprisingly few people know how to relax.

Breathe Deeply

WHEN YOU ARE STRESSED, breathing tends to be rapid and shallow, which further increases tension. In contrast, slow deep breathing automatically relaxes you.

Even a few minutes of deep breathing will produce a noticeable change in your tension level. Deep breathing can be used anytime and any place. Several deep breaths just before a difficult situation are calming and increase feelings of control, for example.

Relax Muscles Directly

ANOTHER EFFECTIVE WAY to release stress is by alternately tensing and relaxing each muscle, one by one. You may have used this technique to go to sleep. If not, try it tonight.

Here's what to do. While lying in bed, first tense, and then relax each muscle. Begin with the toes, move up the legs, through the torso and shoulders; then tense and relax the hands and arms, and, finally, the neck and face muscles. When you finish, you will feel relaxed.

Used often, tensing and relaxing muscles has great benefits. For example, while doing the exercise, dispassionately observe the sensation in each muscle when it is tensed and then compare that sensation to how the muscle feels when it is relaxed. This comparison process develops your ability to discriminate between the two sensations, which helps you detect tension at an early stage. Tension-detection ability is important. Many people think they know when they are tense or relaxed. But the fact is we can be chronically tense and yet be unaware of it.

Develop Rituals

MANY OF US BRING WORK WORRIES HOME us. Even though you may be home or at a movie with a friend, your mind is still working away. You may as well be at the office!

Janice, for example, says, "My job is really stressful. I hardly have time to catch a breath all day. By the time I get home at night I'm so keyed up. I just can't get the job out of my head. I just keep right on working—mentally that is.

Janice compounds the demands of her job by taking on more and more projects, thereby building anxiety and stress even more. She has no time between meetings and other demands to recover. Janice could help herself with a simple technique called decompression. As the name suggests it is designed to create a release from pressure or compression.

Decompression Routine

DECOMPRESSION IS REALLY QUITE SIMPLE. Develop a ritual or routine that you use each day to unwind from work. It can be anything that you find enjoyable and gets your mind off of your job. Reading, engaging in hobbies and doing things with friends or family are popular. If you love to cook, stopping at your local green grocer to select the freshest vegetables for dinner might be a good way to unwind. Don't rush through shopping. Instead, think of it as an end in itself. Take time. Savor the smell of anise in the vegetable isle. Enjoy the perfect beauty of a ripe apple.

The key factor in decompression is the routine. Routine creates structure. It marks the time of the day. Walking the dog is a good example. William walks his little dog, Tucker, every evening at 5 p.m.—rain or shine. Walking Tuck denotes the end of working and the beginning of evening. Routine helps other people honor William's boundaries, as well.

Developing a routine is a form of conditioning and that's why breaking a routine is so difficult—because we're conditioned to feel and act in certain ways. Usually we're not aware of learning routines until they've become entrenched habits. Sometimes routines are good habits that help us do what we want to do—but not always.

Intermittent breaks for renewal, we have found, result in higher and more sustainable performance. The length of renewal is less important than the quality. It is possible to get a great deal of recovery in a short time—as little as several minutes—if it involves a ritual that allows you to disengage from work and truly change channels. That could range from getting up to talk to a colleague about something other than work, to listening to music on an iPod, to walking up and down stairs in an office building. While breaks are countercultural in most organizations and counterintuitive for many high achievers, their value is multifaceted

—Tony Schwartz &
Catherine McCarthy

The idea behind decompression is to deliberately train ourselves in a helpful habitual routine. This is how it works. Select a situation, then always act in certain way when in that situation. Eventually the situation will take on the power to trigger the feelings and behaviors we want. Returning to the example with William, has been walking Tucker every evening for over four years. Walking Tucker has become a trigger for unwinding from the pressure of writing, and turning his mental focus onto evening social activities.

Be Systematic

DEVELOPING A ROUTINE is difficult in the beginning
when you're just starting. You must be very delib-
erate in establishing the activities of your decompression routine. The essential idea is to create
an association (new neural pathway) between
being in the situation and a particular activity and
mood state. As the routine becomes a routine you
will find yourself feeling like doing it. Then when
you engage the routine it will trigger feelings and
actions and you will have created a habit.

When William first began walking Tucker,
he his mind was still back at his desk with his
thoughts going a mile a minute. He cured this
problem by listening to motivational tapes while
walking. The tapes blocked out his work worries
by substituting the inspiring talk on the tape. The
motivational message was uplifting so that William always returned from walking Tucker filled
with enthusiasm and in a good mood.

Exercise

AN EXERCISE ROUTE is a natural decompresser. Just
by getting your muscles into motion, you release
tension and burn fat. When you exercise your
brain manufactures endorphins which like a natural
opiate are soothing. Exercising on the way home
from work, can have very beneficial returns.

Starting to exercise and establishing a routine are both tough and take discipline to set up.
Make it easy for yourself. Find a gym somewhere
along your route home so that you don't have to
go out of your way to go there. Be creative! Rent

a locker where you can keep a change of clothes, for example. Then you can shower after your workout and step right into your evening outfit, ready for a dinner date or night at the movies. If you're worried in the morning, you can stop off at the gym to work it off. In fact, morning exercise is a great routine for starting your day off right.

Laugh a Lot

LAUGHTER IS A STRESS BUFFER, but as with relaxation, the dynamics remain a mystery to medical science. Humor is a powerful tool for breaking out of paralyzing paradox, allowing us to look from a different vantage point to gain a new perspective and release tension.

And we should consider every day lost on which we have not danced at least once. And we should call every truth false which was not accompanied by at least one laugh.

—Nietzsche

When you catch yourself taking things too seriously, use this as a signal to laugh. Think of the "cosmic chuckle" and of the absurdity of our human condition. Satirize your dilemma. Imagine yourself in a Charlie Chaplain script. As a discipline, practice seeing humor in disaster. You'll find freedom there.

Build Community

A STRONG SOCIAL SUPPORT SYSTEM is a stress buffer. The dynamics of how relationships impact on health are a mystery. Perhaps it is because family, friends, colleagues, and co-workers can provide encouragement, sympathetic ears, and feelings of acceptance and belonging. Mounting research indicates that people with strong social relationships tend to live longer, get sick less often, and report they are happier than those lacking satisfying relationships. Pets count, by the way. Research has shown that relationships with pets yield the same healthful benefits.

In a longitudinal study of doctors that began in 1946 when they were students, Caroline Thomas of Johns Hopkins University School of Medicine correlated extensive physical, demographic, and psychological data with the incidence of disease and death. Her mid-term results indicated that health and longevity are significantly higher among those respondents who have stamina. Stamina is resilience and the strength to withstand disease, fatigue, and hardship.

Thomas believed that an open, flexible approach to life; self-esteem; a spontaneous, outgoing temperament; and a minimum of tension, depression, anxiety, and anger while under stress are important elements in the development of stamina. The doctors in her study with stamina grew up in homes that provided emotional support, acceptance, understanding, and love. In fact, Thomas says, "bodily contact of all sorts is very important, especially hugs" in promoting health and stamina.

So make building and maintaining strong supportive relationships a priority. Not only do they feel good and provide a context for a full life, but also supportive relationships fortify against the stress of change.

15

Prepare for Change

F EELING THAT YOU ARE IN CONTROL—a sense of personal power—is the most potent stress buffer. It is the ability to influence what happens to us, which significantly reduces the detrimental consequences of stress. An effective method of increasing such feelings of power and control is to prepare for change.

> *Don Juan: Things don't change. You change your way of looking, that's all... The world is such-and-such or so-and-so only because we tell ourselves that that is the way it is. If we stop telling ourselves the world is so-and-so, the world will stop being so-and-so.*
>
> —Carlos Castaneda
> *Separate Reality*

Consider All Possibilities

THE MOST FRIGHTENING ASPECT OF CHANGE is the unknown. When we make the unknown known, much of the stress of change is dispelled.

The first step is research or gathering information. Find out as much as you can about the possibilities. What ideas do others have for alternative actions and for handling the change they bring? Talk to friends and associates; attend lectures; read periodicals, books, and newspapers.

The objective of initial research is not to terrify yourself with dire possibilities but to become aware of what might be, so that you can develop a contingency plan of action should a particular possibility become a reality.

Brainstorm Alternatives

RACING THROUGH THE BRAINSTORMING STAGE, grabbing on to the first workable alternative that occurs to you, is a mistake. Instead, take time. The purpose of brainstorming is to generate alternatives—lots of them. List on a sheet of paper any and all ways of handling the situation under consideration. Let your imagination flow. Don't analyze the alternatives when brainstorming. Just write down ways you might respond and things you might do. Include off-the-wall alternatives, which are probably unfeasible. This may prompt a breakthrough in your thinking that lead to creative, workable alternatives.

Try on Alternatives

TRY OUT EACH ALTERNATIVE in your imagination, one by one. Play the scenario out to its conclusion in your imagination. Notice the pluses and minuses of the alternative. Notice new changes that the alternative sets into motion.

While watching the drama, be alert for pluses and minuses you hadn't anticipated before this viewing and for unexpected consequences of the alternative. How did you feel as you carried out the plan?

Finally, notice the impact upon important people in your life. You are not an island, you know. If you fail to consider and prepare for other people's reactions, a good plan can be sabotaged by those close to you.

Stress Inoculation

ONCE YOU SETTLE ON A PARTICULAR PLAN, mentally rehearse it, which is an excellent way to practice. You can simultaneously inoculate yourself against the inevitable stress the change will cause, if it comes to pass, with the follow simple exercise.

Again imagine the possible situation in your fantasy. Make sure to actively project yourself into the scenario so that you are a participant in the action. Engage all your senses—feel, hear, see, smell, even taste the experience. The more real the imaginary rehearsal, the more powerful the learning, and the more effective the inoculation.

Feel the Distress

THIS IS IMPORTANT. For a few moments, allow yourself to experience the anxiety, sense of loss, and other stressful emotions that accompany the change, then imagine carrying out the proposed plan and see it working. That is, imagine events going your way—not dramatically, but realistically—and imagine people responding as you hope.

At this point, you will probably notice the anxiety and stress diminish because the plan provides a sense of control over what is happening. You are not helpless—you have a plan.

As Effective As Real Practice

RESEARCH HAS DEMONSTRATED that rehearsal of
new behaviors in your imagination is as effective
as actual physical rehearsal. By practicing in your
imagination, you teach yourself what to do if con-
fronted by that particular alternative.

Further, by allowing yourself to experience
some of the accompanying distress, then handling
it successfully, you actually "inoculate" yourself
against the harmful consequences of stress. The
process works much in the same way as a vacci-
nation, which introduces a mild form of a disease
in order to stimulate the body to build internal
defenses.

Mental Rehearsal Plus Inoculation

MENTAL REHEARSAL plus inoculation is an invalu-
able technique for handling daily life changes and
crises. Anticipate the unexpected, then practice
alternatives in your imagination. If you tend to
worry, subdue the frightening images by creating
a plan for handling them, then imagine your plan
working. This will defuse the fear and strengthen
you.

16

Evolve the Job

I F YOU WORK SOLELY to meet company needs, you become a virtual slave, existing to serve others. But when your goals match the company's, your work serves you as well as your company. In terms of meaning and personal goals, you are actually working for yourself.

Opportunity List

PROJECTS SERVE AS VEHICLES that can carry you toward your destination—accomplishing your purpose. You get a lot of mileage from some projects, others can take you down cul-de-sacs or get you off-track. So you need to analyze which projects can carry you toward your purpose.

Opportunities are "openings" in the environment that enable you to advance your position in the direction of achieving your purpose. Openings are rarely accompanied by a flashing neon sign announcing, "Opportunity is knocking"! Opportunities must be discerned. By taking advantage of small openings, you can position yourself for bigger advances.

One way to start is to identify a range of potential projects and then to survey their degree of alignment with your purpose. List needs, inefficiencies, obstacles, costs and other problems you've noticed. Add ideas you have for innovation, being more effective, and increasing quality and excellence. Each item presents an opportunity. Return to this list often when you notice additional problems or have ideas and add them to your Opportunity List.

You can't ride every opportunity on your list; so don't even try. Instead, decide which problem opportunities move you toward accomplishing your purpose.

Analyze What Is SUITable

THE OBJECTIVE of doing a SUIT-Analysis is to decide which problems have potential to be an opportunity vehicle you can ride toward your purpose.

S—Can I Solve it?

ABOUT EACH OBSTACLE or inefficiency, ask yourself: Is it something that I can solve or accomplish? Is it in my sphere of influence? Can I make an impact on it?

Consider the item solvable if it is something that you can accomplish or cause to be accomplished, even if you must get the cooperation of others or learn a particular skill first. Put an "S" next to opportunities that lie within your sphere of influence or on which you can make an impact.

U—Is it Unassigned?

CO-WORKERS WILL THINK YOU ARE AGGRESSIVE and say you're not a team player if you grab concerns that belong to others. They will feel you've invaded their territory. Even when you have a good idea, it will probably be resisted. On the other hand, unassigned problems are needs, obstacles, and inefficiencies that haven't been assigned to anyone and aren't part of anyone else's territory. Such free-floating projects are potentially yours for the taking. You can take on solving the problem and still be a teamplayer, because you're not treading on others' toes.

Organizations undergoing a lot of change are particularly fertile in unassigned problems. Typically understaffed so everyone has too much to do, much of which is not getting done. Someone picking up loose ends is welcomed. Things move fast, especially during times of expansion offering many threads you can grab and develop.

Review your list of opportunities and write a "U" for unassigned next to those opportunities that don't belong to anybody else or that are already assigned to you. If nobody else is working on the problem and it is not a part of anyone else's responsibility, it is unassigned and available for you to take.

I—Is it Interesting?

THE FACT THAT AN OPPORTUNITY EXISTS doesn't mean you should grab it. Does it interest you? It might help to go back to the self-analysis you did when getting to know yourself, which we discussed in Chapter 1. Review the Action List you created from analyzing what you love doing. Will solving this problem engage activities you love? If so, put an "I" next to that opportunity. Review your Values you listed. Will solving this problem engage your values? If so, mark the opportunity as interesting.

T—Is it on Target with My Purpose?

ONE-BY-ONE, review the needs, ideas, obstacles and inefficiencies on your Opportunity List. Would solving this problem, filling this need, correcting this inefficiency, or removing this obstacle move you closer to achieving your purpose?

Repeat this process frequently. When you see an unattached problem, a need to fill or you come across an obstacle or inefficiency during the routine of your work, jot it down on your Opportunity List. Soon you will have a long list of opportunities—potential assignments that you can take on to shape your job to better fit you, to move towards your purpose.

Periodically submit the items on your Opportunity List to a SUIT-Analysis. Some people try to grab at every opportunity, so that each derails completing the previous one so they come across as unfocused, unable to zero in. SUIT-Analysis helps identify where you can get the most mileage from your efforts while avoiding side-tracks and derailments.

There will be times when you uncover an unassigned problem that is on target with your purpose and interests you, but you don't have the ability to solve it. Having the ability to solve something doesn't mean that you necessarily know what to do right now. Instead, ask whether or not it's in your sphere of control. Can you do something about the situation?

Suppose the situation is within your sphere of influence, but you don't have the skill needed to deal with it. Then the question becomes: Can you get the skill? If so, acquiring the skill becomes a preliminary assignment before taking on the project.

Few people wake up one morning having every skill needed and feeling competent. More commonly we blunder into things, acquiring the needed skills as we struggle with problems as they arise. In other words, obstacles and inefficiencies become bar-bells upon which you can develop skill muscles. If an opportunity problem is on target with your purpose and interests you, it's a good idea to develop the skills needed to handle it.

An early job I had after I'd gotten my masters in vocational rehabilitation was as a social worker assisting men who were incarcerated in the San Francisco County Jail. Twice a week I would meet with men in the jail to discuss how I might assist them during incarceration and afterwards. Sometimes I rescued belongings from hotel rooms; sometimes I wrote letters to judges on their behalf, pleading their circumstances. When released they would meet me in my office, where I would help them develop a plan and give them encouragement. These men had a lot of problems, mostly lack of skills and resources.

I was supposed to do "therapy" but it was ludicrous because these men had practical problems, like where to spend the night, get a meal—take care of themselves. I didn't have a lot to offer.

I began to shape the job. Each morning I would review the local paper, looking for services helpful to my clients. Perhaps there was a flea-market store or a lounge for Seniors. I wrote each on a file card. Then when a man came in for help, I would look through my files cards for possible services for him.

Interestingly, after a few weeks, word began spreading that I had a "resource file". I began getting calls from other helping professionals who worked with men from the jails, homeless and re-lated groups. When I got a call it felt good to have some thing to offer.

I invited the callers to meet in my office to discuss how we might join forces to better serve our clients. None of us had a budget.

When I left the agency, maintaining the Re-source File and meeting with other professionals in the community was presented to my successor as an integral part of the job.

17

Position Yourself

A S IN SPORTS, where it is easier to score from certain positions, so in organizations it is easier to get things done from certain strategic positions. Quarterback is more strategic position than guard, for example. Some positions bring more opportunity; others have more glamour.

Having power helps you get cooperation, open doors and get things done. As Kotter emphasizes, not every position is the same. Some jobs allow more leeway than others. When you have a close relationship with a powerful colleague, some of that power rubs off on to you. Your colleague may open doors for you and you may be privy to important information that you can use to improve your performance, for example. The general goal of strategy is to improve your position, which you do this by deciding where and how to move.

Change, complexity and uncertainty play havoc with our best laid plans. Success comes from continually adjusting your plan of action as opportunities develop.

A key part of the power-development strategy involves moving towards projects or jobs or departments that are strategically important to the organization. Positions in those areas allow one to control particularly important consequences for the firm, and this gives one power.

—John Kotter
Power and Influence

Like chess, workplace strategy focuses on positioning and maneuvering. The general goal in each move is to improve your position to fa cili-ate your accomplishing goals in accord with your purpose.

You move yourself into strategic or "key" positions, but first you must know what you want to accomplish and identify which positions give the best shot at doing so.

Use Strategy

STRATEGY SPELLS OUT where you want to go, what you want to accomplish, or who you want to become. By comparison, an action plan is what you will do, the steps you will take to accomplish your strategy.

Strategic thinking looks at the big picture; not at the details. Strategic thinking is forward looking. What matters is not past mistakes but where you are going and how you are going to get there.

Your life is a path from where you are now to where you want to go. Strategic thinking is employed when you map out a route over a rugged mountain pass, for example. When you encounter an obstacle such as washed out bridge, for example, then you map out a detour. Similarly, when you now your purpose, you can map a strategic path from where you are today, to accomplishing that purpose
in the future.
It may in-
volve learning
certain skills

Strategic Position is key to winning battles. Winning enough battles eventually wins the war.
—Chris Mitchell

through training or volunteering or working at particular jobs. You must take into account available resources and what is changing. EXAMPLE

Strategic Positions

BEFORE ACCEPTING A NEW POSITION or volunteering for a project team, it is a good idea to analyze its strategic positioning. How is this a step to where you want to go and what you want to accomplish?

Information Resource

INFORMATION HELPS YOU have a better understanding of situations and enables you to make better decisions. Having information draws people who need it to you. Information can be bartered for cooperation or access to resources.

Positions that expose you to important information are more powerful than those that do not. You don't necessarily have to have a high-level job to have access to important information. Consider secretaries working for people in key positions, bookkeepers who see all the invoices and checks, or aides working for city-council members.

Identify which positions in your company have high information exposure and what information exposure goes with your position.

Access to Resources

POSITIONS THAT ALLOW YOU to access organizational resources provide power-building opportunities. You may be able to use the resources directly in implementing projects which move you toward accomplishing your purpose. Alternatively, you may be able to act as a gatekeeper, providing access to others in exchange for their cooperation on your project.

Business and social relationships are an important resource, especially if you are self-employed or run a small business. Strategic alliances can open resources to you, because gate keeping and bartering of resources often occur through networks and allies.

Support Decision Makers

THE CLOSER YOU ARE to where critical decisions are made, the greater the power potential of your position. Outsiders looking in tend to associate you with important decisions. But, more importantly, you have an opportunity to interact with and learn from the decision makers. Should a position be vacated or a crisis occur, you might be just the one to step in—even if only temporarily.

Exposure Unassigned Problems

THE MORE EXPOSURE A POSITION HAS to unassigned problems—needs, obstacles and inefficiencies that haven't been assigned to anyone, the more opportunities it affords the position holder.

When departments, or any kind of cohesive group, are in crisis or undergoing rapid change, requirements for qualifying and reporting tend to loosen up. People become less concerned with degrees and years of experience, for example.

The questions become "Can you do something?" and "Are you willing to try?" Action takes precedent over asking for permission to act and awaiting formal approval. Finally, there's a tendency to throw out "This is the way we've always done it" thinking and embrace a "Do what works" approach.

Operating in a rapidly changing environment can be very exciting and fulfilling if you grab and ride the wave. Such environments are replete with unassigned problems. The strategic trick is to grab those unassigned problems that allow you to expand your skills and experience.

Join Project Teams

PROJECT TEAMS are opening a new career path. Instead of climbing the ladder up the hierarchy, people are moving from one project to

Most of tomorrow's work will be done in project teams. Project teams will neither quash individualism nor blunt specialization. To the contrary, individual contributions will be more important than ever. Becoming expert—and enhancing your expertise—will be imperative for almost all of us. . . . Though expertise and specialization are more important than ever, developing "peripheral vision," a feel for the whole task, is essential. You will be forced, routinely, to work/learn any job on the team. Though you will be constantly investing in your own area of expertise, learning multiple jobs and understanding the entire function of the team— and its relation to the enterprise—will be imperative. . . . . . The "project manager" and "network manager" are the star players of tomorrow! . . . Promotions will go to those who are particularly adept at exercising such skills.

—Tom Peters

another. With each project you acquire experience, skills and allies. Climbing up no longer has much meaning. Your experience and relationships are more important.

Support Upwardly Mobile People

MOVERS AND SHAKERS TEND TO TAKE those who help them succeed along with them when they move. Look for positions that put you close to such corporate heroes. If you can't get into a formal position that allows you to work with a go-getter, try volunteering to work on a committee chaired by one. Such strategic moves give you an opportunity to demonstrate your ability and become an essential player on the team.

Follow the Money

POSITIONS THAT GENERATE INCOME, such as those in sales and marketing, are more powerful than positions in supportive functions, such as training.

Get Visibility

YOU GET MORE POWER when others, especially others with power, know who you are and are aware of your abilities and accomplishments. Getting visibility involves positioning yourself in such a way that other people can see what you do.

Sandra was an entry-level receptionist with no college degree or technical training. She aspired to work in marketing, but her weak resume did little to catch the attention of the marketing manager. On the face of it, Sandra didn't have a chance, but she was a hard worker, and had corporate savvy.

Sandra positioned herself to get visibility. She read that a coordinator was needed for a children's fund drive her company was sponsoring for charity. Sandra volunteered and got instant visibility.

The company newsletter and the local newspaper ran her photograph and reported on her background. The news clippings were included in the PR packets sent to all the Divisions. Sandra became a key player in the children's fund planning committee where she worked with important managers and a few Division heads. She gave a pep talk at the kickoff. At the Awards Dinner, Sandra sat right next to the CEO at the VIP table.

By the end of the event, Sandra was known to almost everyone in the company. A month later, an entry position opened up in the Marketing Department, and Sandra submitted an application. As soon as the interviewer saw her name, Sandra had the job!

Serving as an officer of a professional organization puts you in the limelight. Volunteering to head a committee is another visibility position where others can see you in action. Project management is one of the most strategic positions available in today's workplace.

Holding a place on a board, commission, committee that influences the future of the company bring power. CEO of Southwest Airlines was a prominent member of a congressional commission created to chart the future of the airline industry. Put him in the position to fashion the future to benefit his company.

Evaluate Your Strategic Ability

HOW YOU USE YOUR SKILLS and information to achieve a particular objective is a question of strategic ability. Correctly discovering who really has power, assessing differences among people and their roles, and identifying directions of mutual interest involves strategic ability. Strategic ability includes "psyching out" situations—knowing how and to whom to present things, knowing what sensitive areas to avoid, and developing win-win scenarios for getting cooperation and getting things done. Good strategic ability is essential for project managers and others who function outside the traditional chain of command system, such as association officers, fund raisers, volunteer coordinators, and community organizers.

Rarely can you walk into a new territory and immediately be given a free hand. If you want your company to give you leeway in doing your work and to carry on projects of your own, you must develop trust and demonstrate loyalty first. Your boss must feel certain you will complete your assignments. Bosses want to feel that those they supervise are going to do what they want them to do, and not do anything that they don't want done. They are more confident of a person when they know that his or her personal goals are aligned with the company mission, and that the person will not get sidetracked by a personal agenda. As you show that you get the right things done, and do so excellently, you will gain more responsibility and latitude to decide on your own projects and to work under your own direction.

Docpotter

DR. BEVERLY POTTER'S work blends the philosophies of humanistic psychology and Eastern mysticism with principles of behavior psychology to create an inspiring approach to handling the many challenges encountered in today's workplace.

Docpotter earned her Masters of Science in vocational rehabilitation counseling from San Francisco State and her doctorate in counseling psychology from Stanford University. She was a member of the staff development team at Stanford University for nearly twenty years.

Beverly is a dynamic and informative speaker. Her workshops have been sponsored by numerous colleges including San Francisco State Extended Education, DeAnza and Foothill Colleges Short Courses, University of California at Berkeley Extension, as well as corporations such as Hewlett Packard, Cisco Systems, Genentech, Sun Microsystems, Becton-Dickenson and Tap Plastics; government agencies like California Disability Evaluation, Department of Energy, IRS Revenue Officers; and professional associations such as California Continuing Education of the Bar, Design Management Institute, and International Association of Personnel Women. Docpotter's many books are listed in the front. Her website is *docpotter.com*. You can also find her on Twitter, Facebook and elswhere in cyberspace. Please visit.